CONTEMPORARY
MICHIGAN POETRY

GREAT LAKES BOOKS

CONTEMPORARY MICHIGAN POETRY

POEMS FROM THE THIRD COAST

edited by

Michael Delp

Conrad Hilberry

Herbert Scott

Wayne State University Press
Detroit 1988

92 91 90 89 88   5 4 3 2 1

Library of Congress Cataloging-in-Publication Data

Contemporary Michigan poetry.

(*Great Lakes books*)
Includes index.
1. American poetry—Michigan.   2. American poetry—20th century.   I. Delp, Michael.
II. Hilberry, Conrad.   III. Scott, Herbert, 1931–   . IV. Series.
PS571.M5C66   1988   811'.54'080774   88-133
ISBN 0-8143-1923-8
ISBN 0-8143-1924-6 (pbk.)

Title page photo, Ancient forest near Sleeping Bear Dunes, courtesy of Martin Hubbard.

Permissions

Acknowledgment is made for permission to reprint the poems listed below.
Charles Baxter. "Midwestern Poetics" first appeared in *Poetry,* copyright © 1986 by The Modern Poetry Association, and is reprinted by permission of the Editor of *Poetry;* "The Slow Classroom" and "The Photographer" © 1987 by *The Paris Review,* Inc. and Charles Baxter; "How She Knew It Was Over" first appeared in the *Denver Quarterly.*
Therese Becker. "Sparrow" originally in *Midwestern Poetry Review.*
Elinor Benedict. "A Bit of Power" originally published in the Associated Writing Programs' *Intro 14;* "Evidence" originally in *Pennsylvania Review;* "Two Women Leaving Peking" originally in *A Bridge to China* (Hardwood Books, 1983), also appeared in *Helicon Nine;* "In a Far City" originally in *Helicon Nine;* reprinted by permission.
Beth Brant. "Daddy" originally published in *Mohawk Trail* (Firebrand Books, Ithaca, New York, © 1985 by Beth Brant).
Michael Delp. "Gunning" originally in *North Dakota Quarterly;* "Ratman" and "Bloodtrail" originally in *Poetry Northwest.*
Jack Driscoll. "Houdini" and "Elegy: Charles Atlas" first appeared in *Poetry,* copyright © 1987 by The Modern Poetry Association, and are reprinted by permission of the Editor of Poetry; "Shooting Pool at Stedder's Inn" originally in *Tar River Poetry.*
Stephen Dunning. "Something More" originally published in *The National Poetry Competition Winners 1985,* by The Chester H. Jones Foundation; "Homunculus" and "A Sound Like 'Uncle!'" originally published in *Menominee* (Years Press, © 1987 by Stephen Dunning).
Stuart Dybek. "Lights" and "Lost" originally in *Tri Quarterly,* a publication of Northwestern University; "Sleepers," originally in *The Virginia Quarterly Review;* "Angelus" and "Night Walk" first appeared in *Poetry,* copyright © 1986 by The Modern Poetry Association, and are reprinted by permission of the Editor of *Poetry.*
Henrietta Epstein. "From the Shore: Toronto" originally in *Passages North;* "A Severance" originally in *The Windsor Review.*

For Dudley Randall

Spring before a War

Spring came early that year.
Early the snow melted and crocuses took over
And in dooryard gardens blossomed the flower of the slain Greek
    boy.
Before the spring retired came roses
And orange lilies and great blanched spheres of peonies.
Days were warm and bright and fields promised incredible
    harvests,
And in meadows fresh and unscarred
With waists encircled and flanks touching
Strolled the dead boys
And the widowed girls.

—Dudley Randall

CONTENTS

PREFACE

Roethke's Flowers still does business in Saginaw, but now it is only a retail florist shop. If you want to find the greenhouses, you'll have to go to Theodore Roethke's poems—and there they are, manure machine and steam plant, orchids and roses, Frau Bauman, Frau Schmidt, and Frau Schwartze astride the pipes, and the boy up on top, the wind billowing out the seat of his britches. So, too, we hope some of the poems in this collection will preserve the mood and texture of Michigan in the 1980s: a front porch, cool and quiet, in an unsafe city; the Detroit-Chicago train; water witching; a man freeing a trapped fox and being threatened by the trapper.

But in choosing poems for this collection, we did not primarily intend to document Michigan life. We set out, instead, to find the most accomplished poets in the state and to present some of the best recent work by those people, whatever its subject matter. Since we received submissions from many more poets than we could include, this must be taken as only a glimpse of the poetry being written in the state. But we think this sample is remarkable in its quality and its range. The poets here are from Detroit, Flint, and Lansing, and from rural areas in every corner of the state, from the Upper Peninsula and the Lower. They are old and young, male and female, black, white, and Indian. Many of them teach in colleges and universities, but others work as psychologists or morticians or computer salesmen. Their styles vary from understated to extravagant, from closely observed to freely imagined. In tone the poems are reflective, sad, exuberant, outraged, or affectionate.

As the Michigan landscape ranges from Woodward Avenue to the Porcupine Mountains, so the poems written in the state encompass Briggs Stadium, ice fishing, Charles Atlas and Houdini, women drying fish in Zambia before the famine, Eve and Cassandra, a car dragging a dead dog, mothers and daughters, fathers and sons, husbands and wives, a child calling at the door, a crow dance, tattoos, a waitress full of magic and hot sauce, road kills, Ethiopia in 1985, salmon fanning their eggs in Bear Creek, baseball cards, Port Sanilac, and the theory and practice of rivers. We believe this book offers not only an arresting look at Michigan objects and people but, more importantly, a discovery of the preoccupations that possess us here in Michigan in the 1980s.

Charles Baxter (b. 1947) is the author of two books of stories, *Harmony of the World* and *Through the Safety Net,* and a novel, *First Light.* He lives in Ann Arbor and teaches at Wayne State University.

Photo by Robert Chase

Midwestern Poetics

The unpromising meets the unexotic,
and we are home again, alone,
with this image of the possible:
these hills that anyone can climb,
the lowlands, reeds perched with red-wing
blackbirds, leading painlessly
to cemeteries and small towns
where voices are subdued and have no region.
A man paints enormous replicas
of Rembrandt's middle period on the sides
of barns. He is mad. He leaves.

Without elevations, hurricanes, or
earthquakes, without geological alarms,
we learn to count the angles
in the sky and to admire four-barrel carburetors
in the muscle cars that combine with roadside
trees in the six-pack dark of Saturday.
It's not that something has to happen.
A man writes a letter to himself
and excludes the absolute: he is four seasons,
paths in third-growth woods, nature
that is endlessly familiar.

He is a silo: he stores, he feeds.
No horsemen raging down the mountains
flying banners, no vipers, just this and that
that could be anywhere but happens to be here.
The children grow up calm: they learn
about psychotic tantrums like tornados.
They plan. There is time, and more time
and more time after that to learn to love
the mild gifts—these apple trees, these
sparrows—in this marriage with a woman
who knows you, but will not kiss you back.

The Slow Classroom

You could see windstorms and a piece of floating string
making their way to the school
for hours—you could watch the sun,
and the teacher agreed. She had
no ideas either. Everything that happened
took a week in that air, in that frame
of bulletin boards and tiny fluorescent lights,
but when you found a pencil at least
that's what you had, a pencil. They planned the day
for some hours but usually they just said, "Be here."

A plant grew quietly on the windowsill, and everybody
knew it was a good soldier and they nodded hello
if they were standing there and thought it was trying
hard. Where was Hawaii, or any worldly place?
They didn't bring maps. They had a story
about people and what they did, rushing around
in that terrible way they all have
on their business, but no one remembered it.
We were distracted: you could hear

the long arc of water shooting out
of the neighbor's sprinkler and saying, "Why not,"
and you could hear Johnny, my cousin,
who stood at the burnt low end of the playground
stupefied, counting leaves on one sumac after another,
while around him people were busy
making themselves into blurs. And one time they
brought God into the class but all he did
was look at us. And then he wandered away.

How She Knew It Was Over

She knew it was over from the corroded metal
taste of the breeze through the window
and from the silver insects with no names—
the ones with coppery legs and small eyes
like mirrors on the garage roof—that marched,
first one and then many, out of the hole
in the white pine in the backyard,
out of it single file.

And she knew by the full-page letters
people were writing in which trenches were dug
and no one was certain which side was which
or if there was a war; she knew from
the disintegration in trees and the accusations.
And certainly no one was kissing or cared
to make any wine, and then, oddly,
instead of saying, "Excuse me," they

were all saying, "I don't apologize,"
in a rash, low murmur. Then there was
the clarity of breakages, of broken vessels,
hunger and trash: and lectures on the necessity
of children crying quietly off by themselves.
And, as always, there were the men (and now,
finally, the women) propped up before microphones,
waving their arms, telling their terrible lies.

The Photographer

But when I concentrate on what is now in
my mind, what instructions can be found
there?
          —Saul Kripke,
        Wittgenstein on Rules and
            Private Language

1

He knows the tricks for lighting a child: he must aim
the reflector lamps so the face
shades back on both sides, is bright with its
interior grace, its announcement of being; he
aims light at the ceiling, at the floor, to avoid
what amateurs do: to light the child
from the front, like an oncoming car, like
the child's future speeding toward the photographer's
studio with its stinging flash already
out of the case, ready to burst
and wash out the comforting depth
and leave the face a white image on white paper.

2

He knows French. He says to himself, "Les mystères
de peau," and sometimes, "Les mystères de chair."
The trick to posing newlyweds . . . but everyone
knows how you must incline them
to lean imperceptibly toward the warm flesh
of the other and how their smiles must
learn to be solemn: this is a bow
to the world's gravity, this is skin meeting skin
and saying, "I promise." He distrusts laughter
in newlyweds; he takes down their faces
and makes a prediction. "Those," he says, pointing
at four hands, two gleaming smiles. "A year and a half."

3

This began with a woman. This started the summer
he at last lost himself in what he had always
imagined: *light knows nothing*, carries no thought,
is only the touch of a wave off a surface.
He posed her near the window's gardenias
with her hand lifted in what he believed
was a womanly gesture. He stood her nude near
the stairs, nude on the arm of the sofa. After
she left him, he learned to photograph children,
and now at home he says, *See*, as he shows you
a shot of a doorknob, of a dish, of a pencil,
a bowl in the half-dark. Look, he says,

simple objects, the world's wonders, can you believe it?

Therese Becker (b. 1940) grew up on the East Side of Detroit and now lives with her husband and three children in Lake Orion. Her poetry has appeared in *The Beloit Poetry Journal, Poetry Now, The Laurel Review,* and the anthology *Woman Poet: The Midwest.* She teaches in the Creative Writers in the Schools program and is a member of Detroit Women Writers.

Photo by Michael Becker

Sparrow

Androgynous bird,
one so like the other
akin as the weeds of the field;
male and female you blend
the deciduous world.

Common bird from whom
I bribe my cats
with chicken livers and gravy;
you thrive in all I abandon,
a house, an old barn,
the dense coniferous thickets.

Survivor of winter
I watch your tense body
replace its weight
each day at my window,
amazed the small chain still holds
the weight of your hunger,
withstands the fight in your wing
as you vie for a perch to feed on.

All that we cannot name
we call sparrow,
would hardly notice
if not for the confused flight,
crash at the window;
if not for the winter.

At the Table behind Me
for Bob

a man is crying; his small
   daughter is comforting him.
I know this because my husband
    has told me. My husband wants

me to turn and look but I cannot;
   instead, I look forward
into the faces peering out
    from behind him. I search

for clues to the story, happening
   at this very moment,
while I am eating chajitas
    at my favorite restaurant.

The music is playing
   a holiday song.
I have grown tired
    of the loud litany of divorce

at the table beside us.
   So many seem locked
in their chatty circles;
    yet a woman, a man, a couple,

will not say a word to each other;
   they are seated
side by side and directly behind
    my husband's vision.

Their faces cannot reveal
   the food, the music,
what my husband is about to describe;
    a child's small hand resting

on her father's shoulders.
   She runs her hands across them
pats him like a small child
    strokes his arm, whispers

into his ear soft as a kiss,
   while young lovers continue
to sip margaritas,
     gaze into each other's eyes.

The meal is almost over
   when my husband tells me
the man has started crying again,
     and the child, we assume

is his daughter, has moved
   even closer now.
They have both stopped eating.
     I know this only

because my husband cannot keep
   what he sees inside;
yet his face, so like
     all the other faces

cannot reveal the unfolding
   story: but his blue eyes,
eyes that usually wander like water
     over and around people

like pebbles in a stream,
   keep centering
on the father and child behind me,
     lost in this garish room.

It's as if I am blind
   and must see through the pools
in his eyes: the life surrounding
     each life, the face behind

each face standing
   speechless in a world
we beg to interpret.
     We wonder what happened

to leave them alone at this table
   without mother, a woman or wife.

I say perhaps it's divorce,
    and the father is visiting his child

alone for the first time.
  My husband suggests the woman has died,
and I wonder why I was blind
    to the final separation—

death, divorce: brother and sister
    in a world of separations.
Everyone appears comfortable
    at their designated table,

continues to eat in silence.
  My husband's eyes now blur
like an unfocused screen
    on the table behind me,

as some death reaches back
    through this loud world,
bringing the largest of men
    to his knees, humble and lost

in the arms of a child.
  The tables begin to refill
with hungry diners.
    I steal a glance as we turn to leave.

They have resumed their meal.
  She looks like every pretty
seven-year-old who is the center
    of her father's world.

Their ordinary postures
    appear brilliant
in the silence
    still fresh between them.

Elinor Benedict (b. 1931), editor of *Passages North*, came to
Michigan ten years ago by way of Tennessee and Ohio. She has
published two chapbooks of poetry, *Landfarer* and *A Bridge to
China*, and her fiction has appeared in *Mademoiselle* and *Moving
Out*.

A Bit of Power

Keep still.
Breathe hardly at all.
A hummingbird at your elbow
drills the geranium.

At this range
forget loveliness:

A miniature
medic gives shots
to the troops.

Or a small bomb
buzzes and stalls, a green
cigar smokes itself.

Whatever he is, he's all
whiz. Close your delphinium
eyes or he'll think
they're his.

Evidence

Feathers litter the old cedar swing
where last night we talked, where just now
a hawk perches above it, hunched
in his brown cloak, his mouth
full of purpose and new blood.
His delicate beak shines as I watch
from behind scrub oaks, surprised
he doesn't start up, his wild eye
surely suspecting a woman
looking for evidence.

But his belly's too heavy
under white breast, streaked
like a highwayman's shirt, loose
with carousing. Below, a piece
of leftover wing shudders in wind.
He struts the high walk with his hobnails,
whistling a shrill command. Finally
he lifts and swirls toward the pines
as I come to survey the facts
spread around: flyer
inside flyer, gone.

Later, away from the dark, I'll ask
over steak and news, What kind of bird
would eat his own kin? You'll answer,
chewing, What kind of bird,
when he must, would not?

In a Far City

Riverboats toss and groan under our hotel window.
At two a.m. my daughter and I cannot sleep
together in this bed so many worlds
from home: our snow-hushed rooms, warm
and separate, changed to this stiff
intimacy under silk. Neither of us knows
the other's skin. Hers is smooth, blue as milk;
mine crinkled, scalded cream. We try

not to cough or sway the ancient mattress.
But I want to tell her how this dark
hotel's a buried city of women like us.
In this room we meet and part from our
mothers, children, lovers, breath.
This bed swings like a bridge
over all that divides us.

Two Women Leaving Peking

We follow the evening tide that pulls
us through the railway station's
halls like seawater sucked
into caves. Dazed by the swell,
I see myself among swarms
of fish—one small neon among
swirls of dark silver. They flow

around me like chains, hauling
their burdens from earth's center,
where almost everything sleeps.
We inch toward a stairwell, ooze
through its narrows, fan out wide
to a bay where black trains
fume and sigh. At last we grow

legs, walk upright, breathe.
I notice a woman hurrying beside me
the shape of my mother, dangling
a carp in mesh, its body frozen
in weather. I start to live

in her clothes. My son,
his wife and two little ones
shiver in our upstairs room,
anxious to see me thaw out
the prize, stir a white batter,
heat up the stove—but I can't

finish this scene without seeing
my own son, tall, his jaw bearded,
his blue eyes keen, grinning
beside his car with a salmon
hooked on his thumb. Just then

the woman stops, swings her fish
up the steps of the train as I pass
on to mine. She hesitates as if
I had called her and turns
at the door. We look

at each other like migrant
women of two different tribes,
tending our separate fires, clutching
our skins around us, rising to see
who comes.

Beth Brant, born in Melvindale, Michigan, in 1941, is a North American Indian of the Bay of Quinte Mohawks. She is the editor of *A Gathering of Spirit: Art and Writing of North American Indian Women* (1983), the author of *Mohawk Trail* (1985), and a recipient of two Creative Artist grants from Michigan Council for the Arts.

Photo © by Jeffrey German

Daddy

"One time I remember," Daddy says.
"The time every day I went out and looked for work.
You know, day labor.
Everybody standin' in lines, beggin'. We woulda done just
about anythin'.
Them days, the thirties, we begged!
I heard they was hirin' men at the salt mines, loadin' salt
onto the railroad cars. I got there at the right time, cause
no sooner had I signed my name on the paper, I was called
into the yard. I was lucky that day.
Some men, they was usually white, they got to mine the salt.
Go underneath and dig it up. That paid the best.
But I was happy with the work. Eight hours. Hard work.
I couldn't talk American.
Talked Canadian, eh?
They asked me why I talked funny. I says, 'I'm Indian.'
So they say, 'Well Chief, get to work.'
Now that mornin' I'd given blood for a friend of mine, laid up
in hospital. We had the same type.
Indian.
The white woman who took the blood, she said I should relax
and take it easy.
But those days, you couldn't afford to relax.
It was every minute you thought about a job,
about feedin' your family. It's the same now.
People think about workin', not relaxin'.
Well, I got to workin', throwin' the bags of salt
in the box cars.
They were heavy. Maybe fifty or a hundred pounds.
We stood in a line, five of us.
The line went up, endin' with me on the ladder
in front of the box car.
Yes, the salt ended with me. I was the last
and threw it in the car.
My arms were numb, eh?
Sometimes the bags broke, and the salt came spillin' out.
The boss yelled and yelled, makin' us sweep it up and

put it back in the bags.
Some of us, we laughed at him.
I remember, his face was so red, and he worried
more about salt than he did about us.
But see, that was his job, eh?
That's the way it was in those days and
it's still like that.
I never knew anybody a union didn't help.
That day I had a sandwich your ma had made for me.
Pork, I think it was. On fry bread.
It was in my pocket, wrapped in wax paper,
but it made a stain on my pants.
You know how you can remember funny things
about the past?
Well that day, I remember the boss's red face and that
stain on my pants.
And the man I shared my sandwich with.
He was a white man, and he was real hungry.
Told me he had a big family, nine or ten kids, I think.
Yes, that's what it was.
Well, I ate my part of the sandwich and was gettin'
dizzy all the while.
I guess the blood-givin' made me a little weak.
I don't know if I can make it for the whole eight hours,
but I eat some more and sit for a few.
Then the boss asks do I want to work an extra four hours.
I say yes! Not thinkin', but still I'm thinkin'
about your mom, your sister, your grandpa and grandma.
It makes sense to say yes to work.
So I work, eh?
The dizziness went away.
I think I scared it.
I got home around eleven o'clock that night.
Your mom, she fixes me a bowl of soup and some tea.
I go to bed and sleep for twenty-four hours.
Straight.
Your mom, she tries to get me up the next day.
I can't move.
I slept for twenty-four hours!
And the worst part is that I missed

goin' out to look for work the next day.
Your ma, she was mad,
but then she wasn't.
I figure I worked twelve hours in two days and
missed out on four more hours work.
That made *me* mad.
I never gave blood to an Indian again."

Michael Delp (b. 1948) is the Director of the Creative Writing
Program at the Interlochen Arts Academy in northern Michigan.
His poems have appeared in *Poetry Northwest, Passages North, The
Greenfield Review, Poetry Now,* and other magazines. His fiction
and nonfiction have appeared in *Playboy, Traverse Magazine, The
Flyfisher,* and *Detroit Magazine.* He received a 1984 Creative Artist
grant from the Michigan Council for the Arts, and is a two-time
winner of the *Passages North*/National Endowment for the Arts
Poetry Competition.

Skinning the Bullheads

It was Charlie Smallenberger who caught them best,
out late at night in the middle of Bass Lake
using tiny silver hooks and balls of rotted hamburger.
He always said you could feel their mouths
turn into perfect circles around the bait,
then he'd reel slow and long,
bringing the Bullheads up over the side of the boat.
In the morning we'd watch him at the skinning table,
how he'd nail their tails down and pull their skins
off with a pair of Craftsman Pliers,
then come down quick with his hunting knife
for their whiskered heads.
He'd shake their skins at us
and from two feet away
you could see out through their eye holes,
and he'd have maybe twenty of them
white and skinned in the pail
by the time he was done,
the skins slumped in a pile on the ground.

All day you could hear the wild cats from the woods
come in to the dump behind his outhouse
how they screeched and snarled,
fought for the biggest skins, the sweet heads.
They carried the skeletons back into the woods
and when we found a place where a cat had finished one off
we always looked for the bones, even a piece
some part of a spine or skull we thought
would give us some kind of power,
some way to keep us safe,
keep our skins on our own backs.

Gunning

My father always kept the rifle in its case
in the deepest part of the closet,
and I used to sneak in,
run my hands up into the fleece lining,
feeling the stock hard and cool
my first rifle still years off.
On my twelfth birthday I listened to my father
whisper to squeeze the trigger
and for the whole morning we shot out the hearts
of Blatz Beer cans.

Now, 25 years later, I cradle an old shotgun in my arms,
stare off into the woods behind the house
while inside, I can hear my daughter screaming,
thinking I am going out to bring something down out of the air.
So I walk down a back trail, six long neck beers in my backpack
until I get to the clearing.

One by one I throw them as high as I can,
bring the gun to my cheek and let it go.
Twice I open them up just below their long necks,
the beer and glass settling like rain in the dust.
I throw and squeeze four more times and when I stop,
listen through the smoke of six shotgun shells,
I hear my daughter back at the house,
her voice muffled, stilted,
as though something had taken a scream out of her throat,
thrown it high into the air.

Ratman

Thirty years the rat man lived
in a basement
behind my grandfather's house,
tar-paper roof, no windows,
only a small door rising
up out of the dirt.

My grandfather would stand
at his kitchen sink,
watching through the boxelder trees
surrounding his house and say,
"Ratman's burnin' today,"
and the ratman would be feeding
old newspapers,
worn shirts, dirty clothes
into the fire mouth of a barrel.

"Ratman's burning today"
and he'd swish his coffee,
tilt the grounds back into his mouth,
then turn and push them with his tongue, mullygrubbers, he
called them,
and then he'd swallow the whole mouthful.

I sat in his kitchen, grew up there
in the summers,
remember the dreams of going down
into his dark basement,
turning on a light
and watching the rats
come at me from the corners,
sliding down out of the rafters.
Once, I thought I saw the rat man
dump a bushel of rats
into the fire,
was sure he held them up,
looked them in the eyes,
then dangled the largest one
by its tail just at the top
of the flames.

Thirty years and I go back tonight
in this dream of fire barrels,
standing at my grandfather's sink,
his suicide hanging in the air
like smoke.
I feel where my stomach
meets the counter,
think of how he held the shotgun
up close to his belt buckle,
let both barrels go.

Outside there is no trace
of the rat man,
no barrel, no boxelder trees.
There is no sign of where he lived,
but I know this ground,
know if I walk out into the yard
I could dig down,
find piles of small bones,
the remnants of old shirts,
buttons, not enough of anything
to put a life back together,
while back in my grandfather's house,
dust gathers in a dream basement
where the rats wait,
big as men, the shotguns resting
easy in their paws.

Bloodtrail
for Jack Driscoll

We moved through the swamp for hours, our hands close to
leaves, dead fern, the hiss of the lantern near our faces, following
the bloodtrail. Twice the blood mixed with light rain, blood the
color of autumn. The third time we picked it up, we stood still, as
still as the swamp and listened to the deer run up a small stream,
lunging, falling three times. We found her half submerged, her
eyes caught in thin strands of lantern light. She came heavy out
of the water, then my friend went in with his knife, slit her from
neck to tail, slid his hands up inside her, pulling the entrails free,
the lungs swinging away in a wide arc, just enough light from the
lantern to make them glisten like a swath of stars in the sky. We
pulled her back into the stream, air and body heat steaming from
the hole in her side. When we threaded my web belt through a
cut in each tendon, pulled her out through mud and leaves, a
half mile at least, like she was riding the sled she made with her
own body, I kept remembering how, when he cut her open, I saw
something rise up out of her chest. A vapor, mist, apparition, call
it some fleeting glimpse of my daughter, or her spirit. When I
came home to her, I found her deep under the leaves of her bed
and pulled them back. She lay face up, a sound coming from her
mouth. She was gritting her teeth, grinding them on some
strange dream substance. I stood over her, touched her to make
sure the spirit was still inside her body, then bent close,
pretended my hand was a kind of spoon and began feeding her
dreams. For the rest of the night her mouth moved and I kept
feeding. Each swallow and her body went leaping off into a
woods I couldn't see. She always came back, settled into her little
girl's body and curved against me as if we were lying on a raft
floating through the swamp, both of us listening for men
following a bloodtrail toward us. To calm her I told her how their
lanterns would surely falter, how they would lose themselves in
the darkness. The swamp would take them in and we would sit
under a black sky, let our dreams drift back, listen to them
circling closer, their hearts beating in exact time with ours.

Jack Driscoll (b. 1946) is the author of two books of poems, *The Language of Bone* (1980), and *Fishing the Backwash* (1984). His poems have appeared in magazines and journals including *Poetry, Antaeus, Tendril, The Ohio Review,* and *Michigan Quarterly Review.* He has taught creative writing and literature classes at the Interlochen Arts Academy since 1975.

Houdini

So much needless speculation about a key,
how you swallowed it, a dark fish,
and underwater caught it swimming up
between your teeth.
                    That explained
the handcuffs, padlocks, the easy picks
inside that cramped black chest.
What puzzles me is your mother,
how you swore she screamed to you from the dead.
In your dreams she was always drowning,
so you dove from those impossible cliffs,
arms crossed, hugging yourself in a strait jacket.

Except for the crowds, the publicized leaps,
you might have been the escapee
from the smalltown asylum, that single ward
where men finally fall out of love
with their mothers
                    You believed one cure
was to make them disappear whenever they walked
barefoot into the bedrooms of their sons, hair down,
asking to be zipped up.

Once, after sleeping late,
the house empty, I stared and stared
at the shape of my mother's lips,
that square of Kleenex almost dissolved, a perfect red O
floating in the toilet.
I don't know why I thought of you, Houdini,
naked beneath the Detroit River.
It was your mother's voice you followed,
her breasts you imagined each time you sucked
those pockets of air under the ice.

That was always your greatest trick,
meeting her in secret
while the whole world watched, inventing easy answers,
not even close to discovering your elaborate deceit.

Elegy: Charles Atlas
(1893–1972)
for Terry Caszatt

When you died
I remembered myself at fifteen, posing
half naked in the bathroom mirror,
that skinny kid whose body reeked of loneliness.

I never ordered the barbells, the nutrition tips,
never sent you that snapshot my father took of me
beside the public swimming pool, arms crossed and shivering.
But some nights I'd open a comic book
to the back page, try to imagine
how you hauled that train
a hundred yards down those shiny rails,
and how a draft horse strapped later
into the same harness strained and strained,
collapsing finally to its knees to die.

Your heart exploded at seventy-nine.
Weakened by the news
I fell asleep on my son's weightbench
in our basement. He does not know your name,
though in a dream that afternoon
I saw someone who looks like him
screaming for help, unable
to lift that terrible pain from your chest.

So much for your faith in the flesh,
the decades of bulking-up
after that Coney Island lifeguard kicked sand
in your face. Atlas,
I do not believe any god ever hoisted the world
the way you did the back end of a Chevrolet in 1941.
That was enough,
nearly the impossible as we saw it,
that bunch who one day grabbed a bumper together,
each of us flexing, expanding our chests
as if we might call you,
the only witness to our grunts and moans,
the enormity of our growing up.

Shooting Pool at Sledder's Inn

It's true
that my father ran the table
three games in a row on the break,
then took the cue ball, and walking away
tossed it from his one small hand to the other,
watched the white arc blur in the dark mirror
behind the bar.
                    I remember
finding him there,
my mother waiting outside in the car
and how he lifted me into the smoky air
to meet him face to face,
saying nothing,
and those men he had beaten all night at pool
turned suddenly back to their beers
as people do
when it's past getting even.

They, too, knew the single high beam
shining through the window
was the same light searchers use to locate the missing
who do not come home after work from the bars
and who, in winter, simply vanish
out the back door,
the snowfield drifting under the stars.

Which is why I was there,
to protect him in my sleepiness
from any sudden urge to disappear
or in anger, to turn slowly and throw
with all his strength,
the perfect, white roundness of the cue ball
through the silent jukebox.

What I really know is that he smiled
to restore something dying in himself,
the way I do now
slapping down two quarters to challenge for the table,
a friendly game
until it's clear which one of us must lose.

Stephen Dunning was born in Duluth, Minnesota, in 1924 and has lived in Ann Arbor since 1963. He taught in high schools and then at Duke University, at Northwestern University, and at the University of Michigan. His publications include five chapbooks; he has had poems in *New Letters, Poetry Northwest, Plainsong, American Poetry Review, Ironwood,* and *Southern Poetry Review.* His stories have appeared in *Indiana Review* and *Michigan Quarterly Review,* and in 1986 he won a Pen Syndicated Fiction Award and the James B. Hall Short Fiction Award.

Photo by Bob Kalmbach

Something More

If all we have is this, we don't have
nothin, she says. Hey, don't knock
what we have. Some people don't
have this. Well I'm sick and tired
of all we do is this. Take me out,
for God's sake, or get your ass out.

The waitress says, We're outta Bud,
all we got is foreigns. Bring us two
foreigns, he says. What kind? she asks.
God! bring us two beers! says the girl.
It's hard even gettin a beer. It'll be
here in a sec, he says. Take it cool.

I wish we'd never met, she says, wish
I'd never gone bowling that night.
You looked so nice, he says. Your ass
in slacks. See! she says. All we got
is sex. There's gotta be more to life.
You could run for Sheriff, he says.

Here we are, enjoy, the waitress says.
There, he says. She thinks we're ok.
We damn well aren't, say's the girl.
We aren't even friends. We need
something more. We can talk, he says.
Say something first, and we'll talk.

Bambino
(Press interview, Hollywood, 1942)

You boys wait til I take a nip, quiet the nerves. Get the old eyes so
they see. Yes, I'm the Babe, the real McCoy. These movie boys give
me 2,000 clams a week for advice! What do I say? Put my hands
and eyes in your show? My hands catch flies by theirselves. Set
three dimes on the back of my hand, I catch all three in the air.
Last week I say, Put your camera close on my eyes and hands. I
tell em I seen batters blink when they swing. I seen their knuckles
turn white. I read print right off of the bats. I think Swing! you
bastard! I must of made a million batters go for pitches they
shouldn't of hit. It's hands and eyes, at least that's what I say. They
get this cute-face boy to play me. I tell em, I ain't pretty. They say,
Who said you was, Babe? I say, Red Smith wrote my legs was
bandy. They say, Good, Babe, that's good. You ask *Bambino?* It's
baby in Eye-talian or Spic. I got it once in Boston off a pretty babe
sat back of third. I hit one out, Loughran and Weiss on base. I
round third, she yells, *Bambino!* The doll yelled Bambino, she
never made no move. Dark curly hair, nice skin. I say, Find me that
Bambino girl, you got yourself something to write.

Homunculus

Here's his hunting hat. I demonstrate
his round-shouldered walk, trace
his profile here in the dust
on the fender, his Chrysler coupé. Folks,
I give you—my old man!

                  Mon pere tells
of mushing through snow to his chin
Sister strapped to his back
bent to the one-room school. Father takes
me to the ball game and yet
is lonely with hot dogs, pop
almost glum the day Phil Todt trots out
to start his thousandth game
without a miss. Iron Man Phil! Phil
doffs his cap, the owner of MidWay Chev
hands him the keys to a roadster
and everyone stands. "A great man,
that Phil," says Dad, "truly great."

                  Then my old man
takes off with Angie, leaves the note.
I have to go, I am choking to death.
He prints all our names. *I love you
all very much, forgive me, some day
you will understand.* We get a card
that Christmas, Santa riding a deer,
nothing since. Or say he's back, he's like

you, with the hazel eyes? Or like me.
It could be me. I talk about family
everywhere I go, say each time
before I take off on a trip, *You kids
be good!* I sometimes take the boy
aside and say, *Son, you have to be
the little man of the house.*

A Sound Like "Uncle!"

Johnny Boshart's good eye glowers
keeping me pinned. I strain to raise
my stupid shoulders. Johnny has me
down between the cukes and beans

saying what I always say—
Uncle, Johnny. Uncle! I give!
but not so loud Dad will hear his
coward crying in the vegetables

past the fence behind the house
on Hardy Street. Johnny sure
put me down hard. Dad yells
Out of there, son! I told you, you

and Johnny play another place.
We're just now getting beans.
Dad's voice crams the fierce force
of shame up my spine. I stiffen

into Johnny's face. He falls back,
we smash tomatoes, me ending
on top, his head against the stake,
his eye a green tomato, me

savage and strong. I shake
the stake to loosen it so I can
jam it into Johnny's eye, get
some sound like Uncle! back.

Stuart Dybek (b. 1942) teaches English at Western Michigan University in Kalamazoo where he has lived since 1973. He is the author of two books, *Brass Knuckles,* (1979) a collection of poems, and *Childhood and Other Neighborhoods,* (1980) a collection of stories. His work has been published in *The New Yorker, The Atlantic, Poetry, Antaeus,* and *The Paris Review.* He has received grants from the Michigan Council for the Arts, the National Endowment for the Arts, and the Guggenheim Foundation.

Lights

In summer, waiting for night, we'd pose against the afterglow on corners, watching traffic cruise through the neighborhood. Sometimes, a car would go by without its headlights on and we'd all yell, "Lights!"

"Lights!" we'd keep yelling until the beams flashed on. It was usually immediate—the driver honking back thanks, or flinching embarrassed behind the steering wheel, or gunning past, and we'd see his red taillights blink on.

But there were times—who knows why?—when drunk or high, stubborn, or simply lost in that glide to somewhere else, the driver just kept driving in the dark, and all down the block we'd hear yelling from doorways and storefronts, front steps, and other corners, voices winking on like fireflies: "Lights! Your *lights!* Hey, lights!"

Lost

I remember, though I might have dreamed it, a radio show I listened to when we lived on Eighteenth Street above the taxidermist. It was a program in which kids phoned the station and reported something they'd lost—a code ring, a cap gun, a ball, a doll—always their favorite. And worse than lost toys, pets, not just dogs and cats, but hamsters, parakeets, dimestore turtles with painted shells.

I'd tune to the program by accident, then forget about it, and each time I rediscovered it made me feel as if I was reliving the time before. The lost pets would always make me think of the old Hungarian downstairs who, people said, skinned stray cats, and of my secret pets, the foxes in his murky shopwindow, their glass eyes glittering fiercely from a dusty jungle of ferns, and their lips retracted in a constant snarl.

Magically, by the end of the program, everything would be found. I still don't know how they accomplished this, and recall wondering if it would work to phone in and report something I'd always wanted as missing. For it seemed to me then that something one always wanted, but never had, was his all the same, and wasn't it lost?

Sleepers

A sleeper
purifies a room.

With each inhalation
the bed rises higher,

with each exhalation
less dust,
more perfection.

A vigil light
reflects through bone;

sleep coats
the slightest irritant
with nacre.

Now, in a kind of counter-
levitation, the bed
is sinking into earth.

The sleepers pull their roofs down
for a quilt.

With every breath the moon
swells brighter;

their nakedness
begins to flower;

ferns
leave imprints on their skin.

Stuart Dybek

Angelus

It's the metallic hour
when birds lose perfect pitch.
On a porch, three stories up,
against a copper window
facing the El,
a woman in a satin slip,
and the geraniums she waters,
turn to gold.

Beneath the street the blue clapper
of a switch swings in the tunnel.
Blocks away, a crescendo is overtaken
by its echo, and the reverberation
is passed between strangers.
Shadows quiver like sheet metal.
High heels pace off down a platform
like one hand on a piano.

There's a note struck every evening—
every evening held longer—
a clang only because it's surrounded by silence,
chimes of small change
from the newsstand, trousers
full of keys and dimes
flopped on a chair beside the bed,
the tink of bracelets
as her arm sweeps back her hair.

Night Walk

A light beneath the pavement
slaps against your soles;

in each doorway
a cat preaches sleep.

Despite the same, scuffed moon
bolted at each corner to a listing pole,

every intersection
offers a fresh start.

Sidestreets tunnel towards dead ends
where trash fires gutter like candles,

and wind beats like hovering wings
above the watery haloes of streetlights.

Perhaps an Angel of Mercy presides tonight,
guarding the cross streets,

guiding the choices
we make with each heartbeat;

yet, when mercy is required
isn't it already too late?

Remember,
one shoe must step

before the other;
the first rule

on city nights is still
keep moving.

Henrietta Epstein, a native Detroiter, is a graduate of Wayne
State University and one of the founders of the Poetry Resource
Center of Michigan. She is now the Poetry Resource Center's
President, and is Chair of the annual Michigan Poetry Festival.
She was recently Writer in Residence at the Interlochen Arts
Academy. Her poems have appeared in *The Wayne Review, The
Windsor Review, riverrun, Moving Out,* and *Passages North.*

Photo by Leo Sheiner

Wedding Photograph: Detroit, 1935

There is not a flower anywhere.
The bride, my mother, sits cross-legged
on a rented silk upholstered bench
wearing a black dress, black silk stockings
and delicate buckled shoes.
Her raven-black hair is bobbed around her blanched cheeks,
her onyx eyes look out at nothing in this world.
She is thinking of her mother, eight years dead
for whom she is dressed in mourning.
She is afraid that her bridegroom's hand,
which rests lightly on her shoulder,
will firm its grip on her flesh,
or even worse, slide down
and make its claim upon her breast.
She is afraid of the photographer, whose head
is hidden beneath a wide black sheet,
afraid of what he sees
through the mysterious glass eye that is focused
on her and the man standing behind her.

The bridegroom, my father, is smiling
at the photographer's bidding,
even though he is thinking of the rent unpaid
on their apartment in Chicago
and of the wedding ring, unpaid for
in the pocket of his new suit, unpaid for.
His palm on his bride's shoulder grows damp,
and later a small stain will appear
in the satin panel of her dress.
He wants her to know that he never meant
to let things pile up against him,
he wants her to know that he lied,
that although he threatened suicide,
he might not have drowned in Lake Michigan
had she refused him;
he wants her to know that the promises
he made to her brothers
were the core of his own dreams, not lies
as she had discovered them.

As their picture is snapped
and particles of unearthly light surround them,
the bride, my mother, will feel faint
and drive her fingernails into the silken seat
where later, the photographer will notice
the torn jagged shreds in the fabric.

Then the bride and groom will pass
through an archway to a room
full of brothers and sisters.
In the bride's dark eyes,
the assembled guests will alter,
will lose their wedding finery and become
the strangers gathered at the tracks
of the Hastings Avenue streetcar, where she,
returning home from school
had pushed through the crowd to find
her mother dead on a Friday afternoon,
the Sabbath candles fallen from her shopping bag.

Once the bride and the groom
are seated at the long banquet table,
the rabbi and the guests will begin
the prayers over the wine and bread;
before they are finished, the bride
will rise from her place beside the groom,
she will slip from his grasp
and run to the center of the great hall,
her voice, high over their voices
will wail the prayer for the dead:
"Yis-gad-dal v'yis-kad-dash . . ."
her black-sleeved arms flailing before her,
"Oh, Mamma, Mamma, Mamma, why did you leave me alone?"

From the Shore: Toronto

All afternoon I've watched the gulls
off the breakwater at Lake Ontario.
No one here seems to like them,
how they scavenge,
hover like icons
against a metal sky.

But I am here from another country
not so foreign as the gulls'
and I like their garrulousness,
their joyful noise
and the way they hang in the air
flying and not flying.

A Severance

I will see my way out
quietly, the way I came . . .
The close, dim corridor,
the foyer, a flare of cold light
peels the soft sleep from my eyes
while you dream

a wife

a slow hard house
to carry, like belief
upon your back
that you can own a garden,
thrive on breakfast,
wake in rooms of flower-
papered walls . . .

A wife

can see in corners where a clean edge starts
to tear away, like bark
from an aging tree; mornings
harden into crockery.
Beneath the flesh
what's torn does not break free.

I'm used to dressing in the dark.
We've kept fresh flowers
in your water glass
while you have lived on less
than some men throw away . . .
like that bouquet of lilacs
you once stole
because they bloomed outside
a stranger's yard . . .

Tonight I thought
they might have died unseen,
beyond his reach
scorched in the sun to paper.

Darling, when we part
it will be quietly, without blame.
I will see my way out
alone, the way I came.

Lorene Erickson (b. 1938) lives in Livonia, Michigan, 4.1 miles from the house where she was born and raised in Detroit. She teaches writing and literature at Washtenaw Community College in Ann Arbor. Her poems have appeared in *Passages North, Green River Review, Wayne Review, Moving Out,* and *Woman Poet: The Midwest.* Her short fiction has been published in the Canadian journal, *Waves.*

Seascapes

I saw them at the Tate today, Will,
the Turner seascapes.
They are what I remember of you.

"They're Turners," you said.
"I bought these prints with Donna.
When she left me, I kept them

rolled in my mother's attic
for just this place."
And you opened your arms

to the room you'd built
yourself in Cedarville
each board cut from native wood.

Then you turned your ear
to the Lake Huron wash,
all you ever wanted to hear.

Turner couldn't paint figures.
He never understood the human body.
You never wanted to.

I needed to see them, Will,
to know again something
that pleased you,

to see the pulse of Turner's suns
and feel the reds quicken
the ceiling over

your watery patch of the world,
the place you call
enough.

A Quality of the Visible

When I ask you which dress
to wear to our friends' wedding
you recall

the one your sister Maggie wore
in her high school graduation
photo, blue with a lace collar.

I think about wild roses.
You put them in your grandmother's Prussian bowl.
Pollen and petals fell through the night.

You said
"When you look like your mother,
I'll stop loving you."

But I knew, already,
you saw your own mother's hands
when I brought you the bowl.

Tonight I will wear blue,
and as we bend together
through a room full of flowers

you will see in me the moment
when our sons were babies,
my face sweet with surprise.

Mother Speaks the Back-home Blues

Don't you be coming
in my front door

son, my son, my son

with your black bags full
of laundry and books
saying

"I need my room again."

Don't you be bringing
your two degrees and no job here
your hungry friends
for chicken and rice.

Don't you be leaving
your math theorems on the table
wet towels on the bathroom floor
dishes in the sink
your girlfriends' shoes
under the couch
Penthouse under the bed.

Don't you be giving out
this phone number
to long-distance lovers
who call after midnight.

Don't you be prowling
my house at 2:00 a.m.
turning on the lights
turning up the heat
turning up the stereo
opening cans
of Hormel chili, hot.

Don't you be sleeping
here until noon every weekend
with a different woman.

Don't you be expecting
me to remember their names.
Don't you be asking
for the key to my car
and drive through five counties
on my full tank.

Don't you be saying
I haven't done enough
haven't given you a new car
haven't sent you to Scotland
haven't bought you
a computer
a new suit
Christian Dior shirts, 36 sleeve
stamps to mail your letters
yoghurt.

Son, oh my son

don't you be filling my house
moving my things
walking into my sleep
cornering my mind.

Don't you be telling me
I don't want to learn
I'm not interested in ideas
I'm not well rounded.

Don't you be pushing me
to hear you.

Don't you be wanting
me to talk when you
want to talk, and

don't you be saying
"shut up, shut up."

Don't you be wanting
me to expect your voice

to want you here
to need you.

Son, son, oh my son

don't you crawl back under
my heart.

Linda Nemec Foster (b. 1950) was born near Cleveland, Ohio, and moved to Michigan in 1968. After living in Detroit for many years, she now lives in Grand Rapids. Her poems have been published in *Poetry Now, Nimrod, Tendril, The Worcester Review, Milkweed Chronicle,* and *University of Windsor Review.* In 1984 she was awarded a Creative Artist grant by the Michigan Council for the Arts; in 1986 she won the grand prize in the American Poetry Association's open competition. A chapbook of her prose poems, titled *A History of the Body,* was published in 1987.

Photo by Bill Welch

Zambia: Women Drying Fish

In the picture, there are two of them.
Strong, brown, their hands
casually sort the silver rows
of Kapenta fish as if no other
world existed beyond this table
of dried reeds, the southern shore
of Lake Tanganyika at their feet.

Each woman has a small child
slung at her side, kept in place
by green swatches of linen.
The child on the right, an infant,
has fallen asleep while nursing
at his mother's engorged breast.
The milk dribbles past his open mouth,
past the green linen,
anoints the fish drying in the sun,
becomes another part of the landscape.

And what's beyond that sapphire sky
if you could peel it away?
Even the great mind of God
could not imagine the impossible:
a brittle brown twig resembling a girl.
Her black hair has turned
burnt orange, her mouth begins
to fill itself with dust.
And her hollow eyes reflect nothing
but the lights from hundreds
of lanterns on fishing canoes
as they circle the silver Kapenta
lying just below the surface.

The Third Secret of Fatima

She knows it has nothing to do with the end
of the world. Angels blowing trumpets. Plaster statues
of the Virgin weeping salt tears. Whore of Babylon,
dressed in purple and scarlet, alone in the desert.

Nothing to do with the number of days left
to us: as unreliable as the number of rooms
in heaven. Or the color of their walls, or if
they have windows facing west. She's convinced

that the secret is ordinary. Like something in her life
she's forgotten. The exact architecture of her face
as she fades into sleep. Whether or not she is happy.
As she plants the garden, still no clue. Only

dirt; a disconcerting sense of growth where she
least expects it. At the edge of the garden,
her daughter appears almost unnoticed. She
holds a fist of wildflowers. She wears her mother's face.

Lost

Mistaking New Hampshire for West Virginia,
how could we forget where we were?
Place ourselves outside of Charleston
when outside our car it was Manchester.
Mistaking one state for another: pure and simple.
On any journey away from all that's familiar—
beds, smells in closets, even a personal method
of accumulating dust—our minds cloud over
like rain that hasn't quite fallen. A thousand
shades of green become the same green. A singular
blue dominates the sky. And, after a while
(shorter than we could ever imagine) mountains
are transposed without a hint of difference.
The White Mountains are indeed the Appalachian.
Don't laugh. This may not be high drama but
it's serious business enough. Losing a sense
of place is never as frightening as splitting atoms
but for us, lost ones, it might as well be.
We will never find the cemetery where an aunt
buried her seven children. Could be anywhere now.

What the Magician Tells His Wife

Nothing that can possibly
interest you. Dear, dearest.
My sleight of hand, a series
of foregone conclusions I
rattle off in my sleep.
Red silk scarves growing
into white rabbits growing
into stiff peonies from my
thin hands. I am lucky
I do not sweat much.

But you, balanced in a blue
sequined leotard, black fish-net
stockings gathering your legs.
They really watch you.
None of my magic matters
when I chain your ankles
and wrists. Place you
lovingly into the dark trunk.
Casually thrust heavy swords
through your neck, your heart,
your groin. And make you
disappear.

What magic can top the audience's
own, when, for that longest
of split-seconds, they feel you
consumed by the very air. Breathe
you in, allow their bodies
to possess you before I
bring you back—
unchained, whole, visible.

The black curtain trembles
as you materialize.

A Horse under a Sky

You first paint the amber-red
mare. The color of dark blood.
You then invent a yellow sky and
the short bursts of her breath
reaching to the edge of the paper
which has no line of horizon.

The horse seems to fly
in this rectangular universe:
hooves extended, mere hint of brown
wings. Steam rises from her back
and she waits. Hopes for green
hay, apples, the movement of your
small hand on the page.

Son, this is a picture
of the world before you were born.
One flying horse suspended
under one yellow sky. No visible
line of land to touch down on.
No idea of direction, destination,
of coming from, or going to.
Only solid space, blank
and shining. Totally yours.

Alice Fulton (b. 1952), author of *Dance Script with Electric Ballerina* (1983) and *Palladium* (1986), lives in an old farmhouse north of Ypsilanti. Her poetry, essays, and reviews have appeared in *The New Yorker, Poetry, The Yale Review, Parnassus,* and *Poetry East.* She has received fellowships from the Provincetown Fine Arts Work Center, the Michigan Society of Fellows, the Michigan Council for the Arts, and the Guggenheim Foundation. A winner of the 1982 Associated Writing Programs Award, the 1985 National Poetry Series Competition, the Poetry Society of America's Consuelo Ford and Emily Dickinson awards, the Reilke Award, and the Academy of American Poets Prize, she is the William Wilhartz Assistant Professor of English at the University of Michigan.

Photo by Hank Deleo

The New Affluence

Let me say "we" for I am not alone in this
desire to live
where the land is neither dramatically flat
nor high, where it snows enough
to keep the world
the bitter white of aspirin.

People with such needs grew up
snow-belted, rust-belted,
in towns like mine, where muscle
cars dragged down Main Streets
and the fountain's aigrettes outside
the Miss Troy Diner offered welcome
hits of pink and blue in a landscape
largely the noncolor of lard.

Our choice: to love or hate
the slight reprieves from plainness: the fractious birds,
the scrappy trees, and most of all
the things that didn't live or breathe—
factories tearing up the sky with smoke,
tugboats sweet as toys
along the poisoned river.
A budget, if not famine, our lives.
Perhaps a sweepstakes, with prizes so slight
no one cared to enter. We wouldn't have become
susceptible to the tag ends, seconds,
as-is of experience, given better
scenery. We wouldn't have gotten this idea
that happiness is mined like ore from rock,
through efforts of imagination. We, the poor,
but not in spirit, we
the not especially blessed,
who, working cold hours at dull jobs,
drank, gambled, went mad, or grew
anomalous as water—
a compound that expands while freezing.

Disciples of steam and dust,
we take pleasure in considering
the glaciers beginning

in the clouds, the picnic springing up
around the subatomic
particles others call the vacuum.
Our sensory thresholds—the nerve centers
that decide what to let us know—let us know
too much, which makes us terrible
at parties: we seize upon the slight
conflicting tics in idle chitchat,
the wayward rift behind a smile.
It's exhausting, and a social hindrance.
Twitchers, fainters, cringelings,

I'm here to say you'd like it
where I live. In this converted bakery
everything's left to the imagination:
the golden smell of molten sugar, the customers
gazing at pastries baked from scratch
into planes and turrets
fanciful as women's hats.
A tub of lard, sealed and dated 1900,
was the one remaining trace
of baking and we left it
sealed, imagining a cache
of rancid snow within.
The local paper gives advice to liven up our days:
"Colored towels add eye-spice. Look for cotton
run-on sales. A blub-blub of vinegar
adds zip to many dishes. Try it, it's terrif."

It was the absence of spectacular views that made us
see the sparrow hopping warily,
as if the ground were strewn with acid.
(Medieval legend says it hissed
"He lives," to Roman soldiers at Calvary,
for which God bound its feet forever
with supernatural string.)
Lacking diversions, we've turned furtive
in order to observe it. We toss crumbs
while light pours crisp as seltzer, as peppermint
oil through air.

The hyacinths need these cold weeks
to grow into fragrant vases

full only of themselves, their particular
being, like everything else.
So summer comes
to meet us. Soon children
will sell chances on rocks and leaves
from sidewalk stands.
Children! They think these things
are valuable. And we always buy.

Nugget and Dust

My father clipped coupons at the kitchen table,
his numismatic faith burnished like currency
in the safe. He was able
to give himself in visible ways: my birth-
day present, the Buick
Skylark, the silk
he wrapped us in against neuralgia, loyalties
moral as 11th-hour tales
in *True*, the only magazine he took.
Meanwhile, I was full of prim
insurrections, a maximalist
on a shoestring. How could I

admit I withdrew from him
as from a too-gentle thing I wanted to live
forever? I couldn't stand the forthcoming
sadness. Love, if true, is tacit.
It accumulates, nugget and dust, arcade of sweet
exchange. I argued the self-
evidence of all enhancements.
Yet we were camouflaged. I told lies
in order to tell the truth,
something I still do. It was hard

to imagine a world in tune
without his attention
to its bewildering filters, emergency
brakes, without his measured tread. Diligent world,
silly world! where keys turn and idiot lights
signal numinous privations.

Dan Gerber lives with his wife, Virginia, on Thousand Moon Lake near Fremont. His poems and stories have appeared in *Playboy, Sports Illustrated, The New Yorker, New Letters,* and *The Georgia Review.* He has published two novels, a nonfiction narrative, and four volumes of poetry, the most recent of which is *Snow on the Backs of Animals* (1986). *Grass Fires,* a book of stories, appeared in 1987.

Photo by Paul Burk

Incident at Three Mile Road

Last night as I stopped at a crossroads, a pickup sped past, and in my headlights I saw something horrible, a dog being dragged by its neck, skidding over the pavement like a broken toy. A mile down the road I pulled the truck over. "You're dragging a dead dog," I shouted. He was an old man with wild hair and thick glasses. The sticker on his bumper said, *Happiness Is Knowing You're Going to Heaven.* The dog was torn open, the bones and membrane of its shoulder exposed, its paws bloody where it must've tried to keep up with the dumb force dragging it into the dark. "I couldn't feel nothin'" the man said. "I don't even like dogs. This rig's been my home for three years. I travel around preaching the gospel."

And then I saw the dog was still alive, a pup not more than six months. It lay quiet, like a good dog, and I stroked its ears. I didn't want to see the other side, the side underneath where its body met the road. Its eyes followed my hands as I reached down with my pocket knife and cut the cord from its neck. "Somebody musta tied it there," the man said. "I musta dragged it three miles."

Later the sheriff came. "Didn't you know he was there?" He was looking at me, and I knew how he felt. "It isn't my truck," I said. "Why don't you put him away?" I stroked the dog's ears one more time. I wanted him to know some tenderness. "Gentlemen, please step aside." The sheriff drew his gun. I turned away as he fired, again and then again. The dog kicked spasmodically, rolled on its back and howled, the only sound I heard him make, like a woman crying over a child. "Aw come on," the sheriff pleaded. "Don't make me do it again." He fired once more. The dog's legs took one final stride against the sky, its eyes glowed in the headlights, and a last breath steamed out against the cold night air. I pulled him off on the grass by the road, pulled him by his ears and tail, all I could grasp that wasn't bloody. "The road crew'll get him tomorrow," the sheriff said. "I drive around," the man said. "I couldn't keep a dog in there."

In 1948 in Chicago

My father swerved to miss a paperboy, turned the wrong way up
a one way street and got nailed by the cop on the corner. He
never had a chance to explain, and it wouldn't have made any
difference. Maybe the cop had been pondering a nightmare, his
wife moaning under the dance instructor, two floors down or his
daughter threatening to leave home if she couldn't go up to
Wisconsin for the week-end with the defensive backfield and a
couple of other friends. It isn't easy being a father; I realise that
now, the long silent burns I caused, those looks of resentment,
ways I had of putting the guilt on him. Maybe we're all that way,
and he was thinking about that when the newsboy stepped off
the curb to sell a paper, never intending to dart into the street.
"Where're you from, anyway?" the cop yelled back, after the
lecture, after telling him to beat it. "Fremont," my father shouted,
feeling his small-town pride as he said it, certain the cops in
Fremont were never thus blind. "I thought so!" The cop heaved
his shoulders and turned away in disgust. In every thought I've
had since he died, my father has forgiven me.

The Life of the Fox

This morning, before a strong south wind moved in to clear the
lake of winter, I saw a fox trying to find his way off the ice,
testing the edges, retreating again and again until he found a
spot that would hold, that would get him back into the forest.

A tree. A perfect tree. A large oak catching and releasing the
wind. A hundred years of life, a thousand board feet that could
become an ark, an oak bridge, an armoire for a queen, but never
again a beautiful tree.

Is it possible the fox may be my father, returned to innumerable
lives, none of them better or worse in the judgement of the fox,
who chooses without question whatever is given?

Should I save the frog from the snake gliding toward the edge of
the lake? Should I save the sparrow from my cat, save the chicken
from my table, stewing in its broth of wine, tarragon and garlic?

I can't save the deer. I start with each shot and run to the window
and realize what I hear is only target practice or an orchard gun
or at worst a death quicker than by wild dogs or starvation. I
can't save my friend from the cancer distending his liver or the
woman who cared for me from the years that have worn her
away, much less the starving of Africa to whom I send money or
those in love with ignorance who will never open up to their
lives.

Eleven years since my father died to the day I found a fox with
his leg in a trap, waiting like someone's red dog to be unchained,
until I got close. I pinned him down with a log and sprang him
free as he snarled and bared his fangs at whatever it was that
caused him pain. The trapper followed my tracks and threatened
to kill me. "If that's what you've decided to do," I said, the .357 in
his holster, the cold blue/black of a cobra at close range, and I
desperately did not want to die.

Three beautiful skulls in my cabin: turtle skull, deer skull,
long-horned steer, white and perfect structures on which no life
can be rebuilt. Add to them the skull of the dog who sleeps on

91

my couch, of the cat who sleeps on the rug at my feet, skull of the woman whose head rests on the pillow next to mine, the skull I feel with my fingers through my cheeks, so white and perfect and on which no life can be rebuilt.

Judith Goren (b. 1933) is a native of the Detroit area. She earned her Ph. D. in Clinical Psychology in 1983 and has a full-time psychotherapy practice in Southfield, Michigan. Over the past twenty years her poetry has appeared in literary journals, anthologies, and one book, *Coming Alive* (1975).

Photo by Eva Calmidis Goren

The Visit

If she came back now
we would be the same age.
I would offer her tea;
we would sit on the sofa
and talk about the grandchildren
she had never met.

I would want to tell her how she taught me to love
sonnets, whitecaps, crossword puzzles,
forsythia, the ballet, God,
and how, in spite of her,
I learned to love
boys and sex and my own body.
I would want to read her
all my poems, all my journals,
a quarter century, half my life.
I would want to ask about the other side:
how was it when the cancer ended,
where did you go when your body died,
is Daddy with you, tell me it's okay
to live longer than you.
But I would only say,

"More tea?" She would shake her head,
take her teacup to the kitchen,
rinse it neatly, thank me, disappear,
leaving me to wonder: if I had, at last,
reached out to embrace her,
would I have touched a solid body?
Or was she now, was she always,
for me, ungraspable, some
trick of mind, a hologram?

Judith Goren

Phone Call from a Son

You call me from a booth
in Anchorage; my phone rings
at two a.m. I'm dreaming
your nightmare, but it's not

a dream. You stand
on the bare face of the planet.
Traffic lurches around you
spraying gray slush.

Home is a dark hotel room,
a yellow bulb in the ceiling.
In your suitcase, three shirts,
a pair of jeans, some books.

The phone lines ice with panic
across four thousand miles.
When we hang up, my chest aches
with the weight of packed snow.

Snow

A man dies.
The kitchen clock stops beating.

The afternoon sky turns black.
October snow drops.

His empty place at the table
is a severed arm.

His wife stares into a cup of tea
the color of blood.

She sees a woman raise her arm
as if to fling a cup, hears her scream

Come back, my god come back.
She pours the tea down the drain.

Upstairs, shaving cream still foams
at the spout. His razor is on the sink.

She smells his scent on the pillow.
She does not want to sleep there.

Friends with wet boots arrive,
bring fruit and cake.

Their words fly around her head
indistinct as snowflakes.

She longs to build a snowcave,
curl in its darkness, sleep.

Foreshortening

You order season tickets to the symphony
and enter the dates on your calendar.
Suddenly you have moved from August
to the middle of next year,

just sitting at your kitchen table
waiting for the water to boil.
By the time the teakettle whistles
it is May
and you have not yet written
a word of your novel;
Proust still waits, unopened,
on your nightstand.

The Tigers are playing the Red Sox.
On TV the catcher looks so close to Home
he could be struck by the batter
and die. You hunch forward,
squint at the screen
and wait
for the next swing.

Reflections

Do you remember how Jerusalem
shone, the stone walls reflecting
late-day sun glowing above us
as we climbed the hill
outside King David Gate,
tourists and lovers again,
returning to find our origins,
enduring the heat to watch the marvel
of a city turning to gold:

the early sun, entering this room,
reflects off your skin
and reminds me of that.
Each morning when I open my eyes
and see your face glow in sleep
love rises stronger than summer heat
and I marvel at the color of your body,
at our endurance, at the hills ahead.

Gail Griffin (b. 1950) was born in Detroit and grew up in
Franklin, Bloomfield Hills, and Ann Arbor. Since 1977 she has
lived in Kalamazoo and taught in the English Department at
Kalamazoo College, where she also directs the Women's Studies
Program. Her poetry has appeared in *Primavera* and *Ego Flights*.
She is editor and co-author of a work of historical biography,
Emancipated Spirits: Portraits of Kalamazoo College Women.

Eve

When the woman saw that the tree was
good for food, and that it was a delight to
the eyes, and that the tree was to be desired
to make one wise, she took of its fruit and
ate; and she also gave fruit to her husband,
and he ate.
                          —Genesis 3:6

They seemed like three good reasons to me—
life, beauty, wisdom. I was not so stupid
as to believe a snake, even then,
in my innocence, as the breeze slipped
between my legs and my soft toes curled
in the new grass. The snake was always
following me, whispering as if he knew
something, telling me how pretty I was.
A woman knows a snake when she sees one.

It was the tree, the thick leaves
fingering the sun, and the fat red fruit.
And it was the unreason of it all:
that we who knew no good or evil
were to avoid this evil of the tree.
It is hard, at two days old, to swallow
such a lump of illogic. That reach
of my brown arm, that pull and snap,
that sweet bite—those were the most
innocent of motions. As for the rest,
there was no persuasion, no connivance;
in that garden there were no seductions.
I went to the man and said, "Have an apple?"
He always woke up hungry. And then
when he was cornered, he passed it back to me
fast as a snake through the grass.

The penalty, they say, was pain in childbirth,
or sorrow, depending on your translation.
For me, with my good hips, it was more sorrow
than pain. You've heard about my boys.
When they came, the man already was

a wilderness, convinced that I
was his disease and his damnation.
I knew it would be hell with two more
like him. But there was a dearer price
for my girls, those nameless absences
who had no choice but their own brothers.
Upon them, upon their daughters, came
the real curse, known to every woman
who ever looked up at fat red fruit
and wanted to know.

Cassandra

My life has been a wilderness of brothers:
the shrill and greedy Paris, who could make
the palace tremble for his taste in fruit;
the stupid Hector, always big and blind
and singleminded as an armored horse;
the little Troilus, sniffling in his bed,
whom everyone was willing to forgive.
These brothers with their monomanias,
their grand obsessions decked in poetry,
the vestiges and whims of tyrant boys.
And yet our lives, my mother's battered life,
my own raggéd and threadbare life, they hang
upon these trite and miserable gods
until they bring the world down on our heads.
And is it any wonder I am mad,
running the corridors that snake and twist
and never end, like midnight trains of thought?
And is it any wonder I foresee
it all in its sublime stupidity,
its monumental waste, calling it out
at awkward moments to the virgin stars?
I am their very sister, and I bear
their madness tangled in my flying hair.

Renascence Reconsidered

It's no circus,
this business of rebirth.
Strip the poetry away and this
is a season of naked things,
new and incompetent things,
a time of prematurity.

It's no picnic, this shedding,
this muscular wriggling free
of the tough old scaley thing
left behind in the weeds. Days
it takes before you're loose,
only to feel fine blades of new grass
sliding across your milky, tender skin.

It's something, being born winged,
except that you're not born feathered,
but rather, bald, pimply, tufted
with useless fuzz. You cannot see
these gawky elbows getting you anywhere,
so what can you do but squirm and chirp,
mouth agape to be fed?

For spring they ought to write
not epithalamia but elegies—
for all discarded skins,
all shattered shards of egg,
all cocoons like mummy cases,
all embryonic tombs from which
we rise, dumb butterflies,
speechless and lost as Lazarus.

The Woman I Lost

"112 pounds—do you realize you've lost a
whole person?"

I turned just in time to catch her
disappearing around a corner,
the edge of her coat, her left heel
vanishing. There is no point
in pursuit; she is already
through a revolving door,
heading for the cosmetics.
I have seen her before, I think:
as I stepped from a subway car
she slipped into the one behind it—
slight, not a hundred-fifteen dripping wet,
a headscarf hiding her face.
There is no finding her now.
But sometime today, in a buzzing street,
I will turn suddenly, caught
by an image in a store window,
next to the bald unnippled mannequin
whose haggard eyes scan her detachable hands,
and there she'll be, watching me.

Carol R. Hackenbruch (b. 1940) is a native of the Detroit area now living in the Upper Peninsula. Her poems have appeared in *The Great Lakes Review, Alaska Quarterly Review, The Small Pond* and other publications. She is managing editor of *Passages North*.

Photo by Anne Youngs

Memorial Day at the French Road Cemetery

The grave held the boy I never knew;
a brother who only rescued me
in day-dreams. Tall and handsome,
he loved his youngest sister best.

Mother pulled weeds.
Father turned the earth.
They planted together.
I would trace with my finger
the names on headstones,
but never walk on any graves.

There was an angel to visit.
Year after year her marble
skirt hesitated in the same breeze.
I would work my hand into hers,
hold tight until it warmed.

When finished, my parents stood,
her head against his shoulder.
Wet, black earth sealed
their hands together.

Heartbeats

1.

Imagine a father holds
his child's heart in his hands.
He checks the color and texture
of that muscle, the function
of the valves, then bends closer,
listens to the story
this heart tells. He learns
the croon of a mother and teaches
his fingers to lock into the shape of a cup.

2.

Mother told me how I once
stopped breathing, two days old,
skin faded to blue. The nurse
held my chest in one hand, forced
doses of air through my lips
until skin pinked and mother
saw a heartbeat in my eyes.

3.

Years later, my heart, too wild
for any ribcage, pounded
like a fist on a locked door.
Heat flushed to fingertips and toes.
At midnight I wait for the fist,
the fire, the door unlocking
to the morning I put my heart
into my father's hands.

Blue Floyd

I am taking the dead for a walk,
my mother and aunts,
their hands tucked into mine.
We are encouraged to move along;
we will have tea soon.

There is a bird,
huge and out of place,
a jungle exotic
houndstooth black and white
feathers, a blue bill.
I try to recall the name
as my dead ladies chatter.

Someone whispers in my ear
"Blue Floyd, Blue Floyd"
and, yes, I knew that,
I had always known that.
Blue Floyd. Floyd. Father.

He stands on the road
in our path;
the ladies cling to my back,
dust devils grow around our feet.

Carol R. Hackenbruch

Lunar Eclipse

Facing south on the porch,
my son and I watch a shadow
ease over the moon.
Fire flies dot the branches
of surrounding evergreens.
At our whispers and chair creaks,
the goat snorts, disturbed.

When the moon is capped,
stained black and orange,
the stars waver,
move and sway in our waning attention.
After we enter sleep,
the moon will emerge,
collect all our small shadows.

On a Bed Framed with Wood True to Its Own Grains

The dogs are pushed
these late winter hours
to signal one another
over and over

and my sleep rambles
on their voices
under the window,
on the road,
in the woods.

Maybe acid snow burns under fur,
gives them a tight edge of impatience.

Tomorrow night
I will chain the dogs together,
bandage their jaws closed,
pen them under the bed.

Sleeping above their yearning,
I will dream green eyes of a wolf,
locking all the doors.

Robert Haight was born in Detroit in 1955, and has lived in a cabin on Bear Creek near Kaleva, Michigan. His poems have appeared in *The Hiram Poetry Review, Passages North, The South Florida Poetry Review, The Louisville Review,* and *The Sunday Oregonian.*

Photo by Carrie La Rue

The Source of Bear Creek,
Manistee County, Michigan

When I last dreamed the bear,
he rose from the earth . . .
                    —Judith Minty

But no one knows where.
Sure, the lake trickles into it
but that's hardly enough.
Some say the springs north of Kaleva
empty there, others, the swamp.
But it narrows like a two-track into trees.
If you could find it you'd see
a fading crackle of brush, then nothing.
They say the bear is old as the creek,
that the creek ripples in its eyes,
that you could follow it into another time
when you were covered with fur again,
your woman and children lost
somewhere downstream.

Ojibwa called him Kechi-Mecko.
They went off with him and found the source.
The burial mound by Johnson Road
is just a marker, no bones there.
Once I took the dog upstream
and found a carcass lying beside the mound,
a torn fawn. I thought at first some dogs
ran it down but mine wouldn't get near it.
And dogs don't take the belly from a deer
like that.

I think the brothers on the farm
upstream have been to the source
but who could tell through that babble?
When I canoed past their place
they were out there swimming with no clothes on.
The older one got out on the bank,
crawled around on all fours
and growled at me.

And remember when Hoeh-boy disappeared,
the lights left on but nobody home?

He told me he'd seen a shadow in twilight,
thought it was a deer and waded in to look.
He thought he'd stepped into a log jam
when he felt the pull on his leg.
He thought they were only scratches
but they looked like claw marks to me.

Then last night when the fireplace glowed
bear rose into my body.
It held my giggling son and romped
around until breathing shallowed.
Blood turned to creek water in my veins
and washed the dust from the white of my eyes.
By the time I straightened furniture,
the room still stale with his breath,
he was gone.

March of the Walking Catfish

able to scramble about on land . . . it pre-
sents ecological problems.
> —Webster's

Pointing like a one way sign,
the first was wedged in the crotch of a tree
but we blamed an autumn twister
that had driven straw into ironwood stumps,
rained frogs a good mile from the swamp
and dumped manure from farms onto the town.

Others were found
in hoofprint puddles after rains,
in clods broken open miles up the road,
in a well in front of the town hall.

No one paid attention
until children started bringing them
home in their coat pockets. Some found,
eyes revolving, at the bottoms of washing machines,
some flushed into the dank corridors of the sewers
where they multiplied.

Slowly, we started to squint
at our drains like headlights on high beam,
started to glance before squatting,
morning paper and coffee in hand.

At the lakeshore
where the tiny furrows began,
we dropped to our knees,
the road opening like a scroll,

then fought back
carrying Drano and lye like nitro,
plumbers making small fortunes, some disappearing,
others returning with stories of whispers in our pipes.

Robert Haight

We woke in the night,
heard their fins stretching into fingers,
footsteps trailing to the dark barns
where our daughters blaze up like trees.

The Hand That Is a Fin

1

I stand beside my grandmother
and son as they hold hands.
Hers petrified in a slow arc
from flesh to stone.
His, on their slender stems,
are still wet behind the buds.

2

This nursing home hangs no paintings.
My father stares into them,
day and night, three floors above us.
He does not hear my son's voice
rising small shouts in Grandma's room
but she can hear now.
She clasps his wrist like dirt.
When his hand opens
there is a crease in it
I haven't noticed before,
a red line
ninety years long.

3

At Bear Creek
salmon fan their eggs as if rocking them.
Later they move below their beds
into the shadow of a log or boulder
and wait to die.
                    One fall
day after day I came back to watch
a salmon swaying to the same music,
his scales melting before me,
the skin darkening slowly, like dusk.

4

One day he is shadow.
The only fight left is his bulk.

The stones of his bed
sparkle around him.
Soon the shadow will split with light,
waterweeds will sprout between mossy stones,
the shadow and stone will blend into green.

5

The hand that is a rock erodes.
The hand that is a blossom wilts,
its petals blowing across fields and backyards.
But the hand that is a fin
strums a slow guitar.
A man stands in shadow listening,
for that moment neither father nor son.

Jim Harrison (b. 1937), a poet and novelist, lives in northern Michigan. His novels include *Wolf, A Good Day To Die, Farmer,* and *Warlock.* He has also published a collection of novellas, *Legends of the Fall,* and several collections of poetry. *The Theory & Practice of Rivers* was published in 1986.

Photo by Bob Wargo

from The Theory & Practice of Rivers

The rivers of my life:
moving looms of light,
anchored beneath the log
at night I can see the moon
up through the water
as shattered milk, the nudge
of fishes, belly and back
in turn grating against log
and bottom; and letting go, the current
lifts me up and out
into the dark, gathering motion,
drifting in to an eddy
with a sideways swirl,
the sandbar cooler than the air:
to speak it clearly,
how the water goes
is how the earth is shaped.

. . .

Mute unity of water.
I sculpted this girl
out of ice so beautifully
she was taken away.
How banal the swan song
which is a water song.
There never was a swan
who said goodbye. My raven
in the pine tree squawked his way
to death, falling from branch
to branch. To branch again.
To ground. The song, the muffle
of earth as the body falls,
feather against pine needles.

Near the estuary north of Guilford
my brother recites the Episcopalian
burial service over his dead daughter.
Gloria, as in *Gloria in excelsis*.
I cannot bear this passion and courage;

my eyes turn toward the swamp
and sea, so blurred they'll never quite
clear themselves again. The inside of the eye,
vitreous humor, is the same pulp found
inside the squid. I can see Gloria
in the snow and in the water. She lives
in the snow and water and in my eyes.
This is a song for her.

. . .

I forgot where I heard that poems
are designed to waken sleeping gods;
in our time they've taken on nearly
unrecognizable shapes as gods will do;
one is a dog, one is a scarecrow
that doesn't work—crows perch
on the wind-whipped sleeves,
one is a carpenter who doesn't become Jesus,
one is a girl who went to heaven
sixty years early. Gods die,
and not always out of choice,
like near-sighted cats jumping
between buildings seven stories up.
One god drew feathers out of my skin
so I could fly, a favor close to terror.
But this isn't a map of the gods.
When they live in rivers
it's because rivers have no equilibrium;
gods resent equilibrium when everything
that lives, *moves,* boulders
are a war of atoms, and the dandelion
cracks upward through the blacktop road.
Seltzer's tropical beetle grew
from a larval lump in a man's arm,
emerging full grown, pincers waving.
On Mt. Cuchama there were so many
gods passing through I hid in a hole
in a rock, waking one by accident.
I fled with a tight ass and cold skin.
I could draw a map of this place
but they're never caught in the same location

twice. And their voices change from involuntary
screams to the singular wail of the loon,
possibly the wind that can howl down Wall St.
Gods have long abandoned the banality of war
though they were stirred by a hundred-year-old
guitarist I heard in Brazil, also the autistic child
at the piano. We'll be great at death
so why should I wait? Today I invoked
any available god back in the woods in the fog.
The world was white with last week's melting
blizzard, the fog drifting upward, then descending.
The only sound was a porcupine eating bark
off an old tree, and a rivulet beneath the snow.
Sometimes the obvious is true: the full
moon on her bare bottom by the river!
For the gay, the full moon on the lover's prick!
Gods laugh at the fiction of gender.
Water gods, moon gods, god fever,
sun gods, fire gods, give this earth diver
more songs before I die.

.　.　.

On waking after the accident
I was presented with the "whole picture"
as they say, magnificently detailed,
a child's diorama of what life appears to be:
staring at the picture I became drowsy
with relief when I noticed a yellow
dot of light in the lower right hand corner.
I unhooked the machines and tubes and crawled
to the picture, with an eyeball to the dot
of light which turned out to be a miniature
tunnel at the end of which I could see
mountains and stars whirling and tumbling,
sheets of emotions, vertical rivers, upside
down lakes, herds of unknown mammals, birds
shedding feathers and regrowing them instantly,
snakes with feathered heads eating their own
shed skins, fish swimming straight up,
the bottom of Isaiah's robe, live whales
on dry ground, lions drinking from a golden

bowl of milk, the rush of night,
and somewhere in this the murmur of gods—
a tree-rubbing-tree music, a sweet howl
of water and rock-grating-rock, fire
hissing from fissures, the moon settled
comfortably on the ground, beginning to roll.

Looking Forward to Age

I will walk down to a marina
on a hot day and not go out to sea.

I will go to bed and get up early,
and carry too much cash in my wallet.

On Memorial Day I will visit the graves
of all those who died in my novels.

If I have become famous I'll wear a green
janitor's suit and row a wooden boat.

From a key ring on my belt will hang
thirty-three keys that open no doors.

Perhaps I'll take all of my grandchildren
to Disneyland in a camper but probably not.

One day standing in a river with my flyrod
I'll have the courage to admit my life.

In a one-room cabin at night I'll consign
photos, all tentative memories to the fire.

And you my loves, few as there have been, let's lie
and say it could never have been otherwise.

So that: we may glide off in peace, not howling
like orphans in this endless century of war.

Conrad Hilberry (b. 1928) grew up in Ferndale, Michigan, and now teaches at Kalamazoo College. He has published three volumes of poems, *Encounter on Burrows Hill* (1968), *Rust* (1974), and *The Moon Seen as a Slice of Pineapple* (1984). His latest book is the psychological case study, *Luke Karamazov* (1987).

Mstislav Rostropovich
(Row J, Top Balcony, Hill Auditorium, Ann Arbor)

Far below us, the curved walls converge
to a tiny circle of light. In it, a bald
man sits, holding a cello between his knees
as a father might hold a child.

He bows the strings simply, telling a story
we all have heard before. We did not know
each other, but everyone on the steep bank
leans together to follow

the words, the working out of the old plot.
It is as we remember it, but clearer,
everything told just as it must have happened—
the knocking on the door,

the gift of a shirt, the flowers, the dark road.
He catches the lift or falter of each voice
and lets a simile unfold like wood
smoke. The action goes

as we know it must, tangled in jealousy, the bird
lost, the lovers misunderstanding. The story
pauses and plummets like water over a rock.
Silence. The cellist reaches for

a handful of high notes—ourselves in the top
balcony! He finds us right where he left us
and plays us pure and sweet as a bunch of onions
hanging from the rafters.

Crickets and the Rain

Here is a truth not everybody knows:
when the rain begins, even this gentle dripping,
the crickets stop. No sound. Except, of course,

the rain itself, dropping wet vocables
under the trees—as, at the base of my tongue,
I talk to myself, muttering old scenes

with new endings, rehearsing what must be said,
suffering again embarrassments and griefs.
Now the rain stops. Before the crickets dry

and rosin their legs, listen: perfect silence.
I rise and hang, a musky smell in the air,
weightless, with no thought for gravity

to catch on. Without the deliberating rain,
hemlocks float up like buoys, their roots dangling,
and porcupines, detached from everything

but body, swim at eye level around
the trunks of trees, through air that can no longer
call itself *the air.* They blink, their eyes

like running lights, but no code passes here,
no understanding mars our aimlessness,
until the crickets bring up words again.

Sorting the Smoke

If all things were turned to smoke, the nos-
trils would distinguish them.
> —Heraclitus

I

In the thick smoke, the nostrils lift
and sniff: cedar roof beams, the soggy
blanket that has hung all these years
in the shed, paint from kitchen chairs,
the singed fur of cat and the flesh
of cat, and the loquat tree by the wall,
and thyme, and books in grandfather's room
and his wool robe and the mattress
and grandfather and the coarse grasses
behind the house. Whose nostrils are
we speaking of, downwind of the fire?

II

The smoke billows in dark eddies
as though the world hid just behind it,
as though it might drift off, and the road,
the child in white, the blind horse tied
to the cypress tree might reappear
like fishing boats still hung with mist.
But no. The smoke does thin and swirl
and fade, but nothing steps out, no shapes
re-form in the middle distance;
only the emptiness comes clear
to the watcher who himself is smoke.
A faint smell lingers, and the nostrils
sort it into everything that was.

On the Promontory

All things are an exchange for fire.
                    —Heraclitus

You can believe it on a day like this
when haze hangs on the islands and the sea
smolders against the sky. Here on the headlands,

the long blue swells ease in from the Aegean,
leisurely as childhood, then churn and swirl
on these volcanic rocks, blaze up

in a white flame, and fall, becoming ash
and undertow. Here at the joint of youth
and age, the genes blaze up, and all

this blue, the breath of a woman rising
and falling in sleep, all this is fire.

Self-Portrait as Bank Teller

As my fingers almost touch the fingers
reaching under the bars but touch instead
checks and deposit slips—as my hand reaches

for the other hand and almost touches it—
I feel the float, the moment out of time
when money passed from hand to hand forgets

the pale depositer and rains interest
on the banking clerk himself—on me
as I hit the date stamp and slide the bills

into the drawer. All day, between the hand in
and the hand out, I sense the float distilling
its small rain about me, between words in

and words out, I hear the silence adding its six
percent, the miracle of commerce that blesses
even those who sign no checks themselves.

Patricia Hooper (b. 1941) lives in Birmingham. Her poems have appeared in *Poetry, The American Scholar, The American Poetry Review,* and *The Ohio Review.* In 1984 her book, *Other Lives,* was awarded the Norma Farber First Book Award of the Poetry Society of America. A children's book, *A Bundle of Beasts,* was published in 1987.

Money

He walks into the cold.
Shadow of elms darken the wet pavement,
and a wind blows at his back.

In the houses the rich are sleeping
in their deep furs. The tall
porches, the black, elegant street lamps
gleam like the aisles of a church.

He has come too far. Now
he notices how he has walked
without noticing, leaving his wife
and the small meal she is placing
back on the stove. He thinks
of her face, bitter and weeping
at his hot words, stares

at the luminous closed curtains
of the next house: a man
has come home to his wife, the lamplight
a star on their upstairs window,
glistening, crusted with pearls.

It begins snowing. Crystals
of ice form on the street lamps
like frost on his own window: he sees
his table, the twin chairs
facing each other
night after night, the room
growing older and darker . . .

                   Here,
in these high rooms, he believes
they could talk to each other, their words
blazing like coins and their silk
sleeves touching, their valuable white
bodies adrift without malice
above the earth.

You Ride in His Black Car

You ride in his black car,
curling your long, delicate

fingers over his wrist. It is raining
in the city, and the street is

silver. You adjust your shawl, you pour
the colors of your dress.

He notices. The rain
has vanished, and you turn away toward

sunset. Now the streets
are purple, there are homes

and children being put to bed. You watch
their porch lamps, parlor windows. In

the last, you see her chair: a woman past
the screen is resting, reading to

her child. The streets are jewelry. Now
you thrust your hand into the cool

night air. It pulls like water. You can touch
the leaves again, the lawns, the streets

you've left. The temperature
is rising. You can feel

the curtains blowing in, the other life.

Scarred

It's seduction
that startles: the scar

where his face was,
a boy's face. Then
the explosion.

Then the awful
turning aside so as to sicken no one.

His hands burned into fringes, his eyes
smudged shut, the hook
of his body.

Still you know
he's met you before with the same
speechless peculiar dare.

It's the come-on, his challenge
not to you but to all of it.

The Ordinary Life

A friend writes, "You won't know me.
I have chosen
the ordinary life . . ."

Reading, I still remember
the secret we once shared:
how we lived for the rare moment
when light burns inward
and the small knot of self
dissolves in a flare of leaf,
the brief, unexpected bird
splitting the sky open.
To have chosen the ordinary—
as if comfort were common
or order could be expected,
when over the rinsed plate
or a daughter's unbrushed hair,
a star suddenly flickers
on the familiar wall,
when curtains are visited
by odd, unpredicted gusts,
and we look up, during dinner,
at a face known but unknown.

Even here, in unmapped rooms,
a tangle of vine thickens
and a bird cries, sudden
and changed in a foreign country,
through whose unfamiliar paths
we arrive home.

Jogging in the Cemetery

No sign saying, *Don't run.*
Nevertheless, I slow down
to keep pace with the dead
who move with great effort.
I can hear their bones

pulling themselves together
as they catch on.
I can tell how they take notice.
They consider the wet streets,
maples ablaze, shops

open across town.
They remember their lit rooms
and thick sofas. They try
shaking the dream off,
the dream in which they are dead

and somebody jogs past.
I feel how they mean to run
with me in this middle-aged
morning amid gravestones
in the mild sun.

Murray Jackson, born in 1926 in Philadelphia, grew up on Brush and Canfield in Detroit. He attended Wayne State University and joined the faculty in 1955. He served from 1964 to 1965 as Coordinator of Special Projects for the University of Michigan Opportunity Awards Program and from 1967 to 1970 as the founding president of Wayne County Community College. He joined the faculty of the University of Michigan Center for the Study of Higher Education in 1971. He has served as Chairman of the American Lung Association, as a member of the Michigan Council for the Humanities, and as Chairman of the Detroit Council of the Arts. In 1983, he was appointed by Governor William Milliken to serve as Chair of the newly formed Design Study Committee for the State of Michigan.

University of Michigan Information Services photo

Growing Up Colored

The Old Boy walking from Canfield and Woodward
to Mansfield Highland Park Ford Plant
with Herman Davis, Sam Rustin
Looking to find Mr. Henry's man, Marshall,
who could say these boys are all right.

Pick up men, duck run between
alleys and houses, not to get caught
to put your number in.
If you guess right, hoping that he
would hop, skip, and jump to your
door with the hit money.

Trying to be the temporary weather boy
Look at the sky, scratch your head
digging in your ass
shuffle at the same time
waffling through a minefield
of egg shells
You Got Rhythm.

Jabberwacking through the pains
and sorrows of being colored
Dancing sometimes,
even jitterbugging
through a Strauss waltz.

Friday night, rent party
was it going to be at Eva's again?
After we could go to the fish fry
at Wimpy's
Up all Saturday night.

Pray a little on Sunday
Stand on tiptoes, straining to peer
on the other side of death,
Singeing the edges of despair
with "Swing Low Sweet Chariot."
Start to be colored again on Monday.

Dudley Randall

Pushed through a crack in earth
your eyes burn fire, soft as soft
your vision of cities: Green Apples, Roses
and Revolution.

You find the green moss discover north
tie square knots to hold our world together
press the pressure points to keep us
from bleeding on city streets.

In Paradise Valley, your man
Caruso flashes the ruby stick-pin,
Stands on his chair
talks about being colored.

Prophet Jones Sashays
to his temple on Hague.
floats to the pulpit in his ermine robe
Hands outstretched for alms.

Casablanca shadows the street
Orchestra Place, touts
his basement palace a place
to look at cards, have
a taste or two.

You catch the mellow harmony
of their beat
siphon time, bottle it, then
uncork and stick it in our eye.

Detroit-Chicago Train Time

Michigan Central railroad station,
ancient Greek temple Doric columns
Corinthian cloisters.
The walls and floors could sing
had they voices.

World War II troop trains from all over the country,
stopping for a moment at Michigan Central.

From the station to the train yard reminds you
Frankfurt, 1944–45.
Twisted pieces of concrete and steel like black
and red licorice.

Yards of junk, pieces of brown-green machinery
Houses that sit and look at you through dirty windows.
Yards back and front stuffed full of cots, chairs,
ovens, refrigerators.
Yes, a portable swimming pool

Fields of corn,
some cabbage,
cows slapping air in search of flies,
horses ogling grass
19th century railroad stations
Niles, Kalamazoo, Jackson.

My friend and colleague, Cleo Harpoon,
working her treatise "The History of Junk," might
find this route ideal for a museum
on everything nobody wants.

Gulls

Yellow nosed Herring Gulls
sculling the sky.
looking for alms on water. waste dumps
even black-top parking lots
wherever there is a handout.

Whispering in the eardrums of air
Hiyah   Hiyah   Hiyah

Moving with the rhythm of a smooth slick piston
in unison with the glide of grease on grease.

David James, born in 1955 in Detroit, works as Director of Admissions for the University of Michigan–Flint. His book *A Heart Out of This World* was published in 1984. He lives with his wife, Debra, and their three children.

A Worm's Life

The earthworm has five hearts.

It would take that many
to love yourself
as a worm.
Even with your blind ambition,
you cannot deny
your best friend is dirt.
For fun, you burrow out of sight
and explore the underworld
with ants, grubs, parasites.
Your body, a pencil-thin tongue,
arches, inches, arches,
curls and writhes in a language
of darkness, of moist silence.
With five hearts, your journey
toward love is suspect.
Since you carry both eggs and sperm,
at once father and mother,
you look for a one-nighter,
time enough to lie around
fertilizing, getting fertilized.
Then off you slide,
never looking back,
never writing or calling,
never a second thought about love.

You live out your life
in a rut, down and out,
slipping through blackness,
praying for no sudden rain.
And on those strange occasions
when you are allowed to dream,
you picture yourself
riding across the open plains,
leading a million worms westward,
wind against your slimy skin,
sun glaring through your transparency.
You let out a "Yeehah!"

David James

The birds ripple into the sky
until all of your five hearts
beat you back
into a worm.

A Timeless World
for Marc Sheehan

There is a world,
not a heaven,
where we place
our fathers and mothers,
grandparents, aunts,
friends.
In it, their figures
are created, jostling
our hair, touching
our shoulder, laughing,
hugging, whispering
a bedtime prayer.
A timeless world,
we may summon it at will,
images casting in our foreheads,
words and voices burning
into our hearts.
This very moment, in the dark,
our dead sit patiently,
untouched by wind or noise,
the routines of eating, cleaning.
They rise and enter this world,
not exactly a heaven,
when we need them and when we don't:
standing, talking, wrestling,
more real
than they ever wanted to be.

The Politics of an Idiot

If a politician has dark eyebrows, his signature is illegible. His
wife has affairs. His children sleep in their underwear only.
And he will not tell you the whole truth.

If a politician has light eyebrows, he owns a bird, but forgets
to feed it. He drives a red car. His house has three entrances,
    seven
exits. His lawn is sprayed with chemicals. And he will cost you.

If a politician has large, bushy eyebrows, he once worked in a
clothing store and was fired. He doesn't know the names of all
his cousins. His golf swing is unorthodox. And he will turn
    against
you the minute he assumes office.

If a politician has no eyebrows, elect him. He is the one who
has nothing to hide.

The Guest in Your Head

Your brain is a fat bird,
perched on a limb,
who suddenly lifts his shoulders
and steps off, sailing
into the darkest sky.
There's no such thing
as gravity here.
With his head in the clouds,
any turn or swoop is possible;
one flick of a feather
sends him into a world
of difference.

You invite him over for dinner
but he only eats fish:
pelican, osprey.
He's playing with your emotions,
headgames, you say.
He sneezes and wipes
himself with brain tissue.
It's like he's underwater,
chewing in slow motion, gulping food,
until he floats above the table,
out the window.
Now you see a fish flying
through the heavens,
pretending to be a brain,
feathery and fat,
swooping low to feast
on every idea in sight.

David James

The World Drinks

Spring is here
crazier than ever.
The morning, sunshine, 60°,
turned to dark clouds
& snow flurries,
& by evening, a rainbow,
a bleeding sun over the trees.
Spring, with everything
on her face,
blows into town on a white horse,
hair up in a bandana,
a flask in every pocket.
When she drinks,
the whole world drinks.
Worms go berserk,
in & out of their rainy holes;
robins barely flying,
fatter than cats.
We get used to testing the air
before going out:
spring coat, winter coat, no coat.
But Spring is here for good,
lying on the grass,
passed out in the trees,
wading through rivers
in her bare feet.
Before May,
we'll be lifting our mouths to the sky
& drinking whatever she pours on us,
in love, insane,
unsteady in our bodies,
every dream
a wet one.

Janet Kauffman was born in 1945 in Lancaster, Pennsylvania, and has lived in Hudson, Michigan, for the last fifteen years. She has published two books of fiction, *Places in the World a Woman Could Walk* and *Collaborators*, as well as a book of poetry, *The Weather Book*.

Photo by Matthew Borland

Wild Asparagus

Over the years, all the extortionists buried in ditches
by the side of Beecher Road, and the other men, too,
dumped at the edges of grassy lanes, their bodies warm
from the trunks of the navy blue cars that carried them,
these inappropriate, anonymous men have pressed their bones
downward, leaving their flesh overhead, a separation they
    imagined
as spiritual, but which they now see as further attachment.
All of them, rankled by the persistence of body, begin running
in place, underground, in the middle of May, in the damp
Michigan wasteland, until with their steadying thrusts, the
    ground
gives at the scattered surfaces and suddenly their sweet,
    low-lying
cocks uncurl, green as the tall grass where they rise, thickly,
tumescent, touching again the air that had blessed them
once when as boys each one lay flat, face up, in a wide field
and, in spite of the sun, each one claimed to have seen
through the layered glitter of sky to the darkest blue,
deeper than water, they all said, deeper than anything they
    knew.

Janet Kauffman

In August I Saw My Grandfather Many Times

In August he speared tobacco, the long stalk,
like a girl in green skirts, lifting her,
balancing her—then the hollow crack
through the marrow as she came down.
On the ground, the velvet leaves wilted
like difficult tropical things, lopped
for the tourists to poke and hold to the light.
Late in the day, when I drove the tractor
into the field, I watched him shift his weight
and lift each lath to the scaffolding of the wagon.
There was an awkward moment, unmistakable,
when he held the leaves in his arms,
against the length of his body, setting his hand
for the last handling; and he breathed in
the leaves' dust, his mouth on the leaves' hair.
Many times in August, the hottest days,
I saw him embrace, like a father who knows his crimes,
these withering girls.

The World of Men

It is out of season—the way things are

in February, when even the gifted Mafia men
stretch out under a palm on an empty Bahamian beach.

They take off their shiny shoes. They sleep.
In the suburbs of Detroit, two boys

put a stethoscope to concrete, hush.
They kneel down, listen, one then the other.

Janet Kauffman

The Man in the Pool

The man in the pool swims backwards.
He draws through the water his sloped, womanly
body. His eyelids close.
Children make way. The young girls dive
holding hands, twinned, beneath him.
Measure, he thinks. Measure.
Small waves, ripples, wash over his brow.
He believes he has kissed his children
many times in their sleep, while his body continues
propelling itself, and buoyant beside him
the on-going dead drift further and further
away from everything they have ever known.

The Child Comes In

When the door opens for the child, the child comes in
because she has wanted to come in and has called
once to bring someone to the door, and although
it is not an astonishing thing, it happens
without incident, and when the wooden door closes
it is as satisfying a sound as anyone
in the house can imagine, more satisfying
than when the dishwasher locks shut for the night,
because the dishes have not wanted one thing
rather than another, but the child has, and
enough attention has been paid, just enough,
and just the right action has been taken, so that
no violence was done and none was contemplated,
allowing at least one event, unplanned, unforeseen,
to occur harmlessly in a world of occurrences
elsewhere that sicken and disrupt and mutilate
and leave whole populations aghast, sleepless.

Josie Kearns (b. 1954), born and raised in Flint, is currently Director of the Visiting Writers Series and Young Writers Academy for the University of Michigan–Flint and a free-lance journalist for *The Flint Journal* and *The Detroit Free Press.* Her work has appeared in *Science '85, Greenfield Review, Kansas Quarterly, Passages North, Crosscurrents,* and *Industrial Strength Poetry.* She received a 1987 Creative Artist award from the Michigan Council for the Arts.

Photo by KEVA

Agreeing with Everyone

At the filling station,
the gas jockey complains about how it is
and I say yeah because I can see
how it is for him
and the administrator tells me
what a mess he's in
and I agree
and when a friend says
But what can you do?
I don't know.

I'm not an apple polisher
but I could see how you'd think so
as I listen like a sponge,
with continuous low blood pressure,
a certain wander of the eye.

So busy nodding
and uh-huh-ing it through life
that I catch a thief and understand
how stolen property is a rude gift
especially mine.

And when I interview the murderer
and she tells me how she lit the bed
we talk about certain aromas of the epidermis
as fine candles and the different qualities
of kerosenes and which burns best.

And when the inquisitor comes for me with a knife
and lays my spleen and kidney
on the nightstand
we talk about how beautiful
people are inside
how the reds and purples within us
are the deepest on the planet.

Aunt Florence

Visiting a relative who has not yet been diagnosed,
it is Florence who gulps down three barbiturates
without water, enters the white room
and says brightly,
"My God, honey, I hope you don't have
a brain tumor!"

She and my step-father once took turns
trying to pull the telephone out of the wall.
I think they wanted to deny each other
the satisfaction of calling the police.
She was fire, her auburn hair curled
like autumn leaves, chain-smoking,
smoke swirling above her head in fists.
While he was a tidal wave, grown mad
with volumes of whiskey, an alien,
his face blue with explosion.

Both survived the hollering, slung arms
around shoulders and cried in the end
over their children.
The son visits only on weeks Dad
has seen the psychiatrist.
Her daughter does not attend family functions.
They miss out.

On her fifth marriage, as the license was written,
her fiance expressed amazement at the number
of former husbands whose names she wrote out by hand.
She paused, glared at the newcomer, said,
"Listen, dammit, I was in demand!"

The Way the Body Starves

The body requires several stages to starve
itself.
                    —Newspaper article

First, bite into blood,
sieve the nutrients.
The body searching in snatches
unravels the energy of dull lumps.
Ravenous, it sections the brain
like a grapefruit.
Thieving protein, it throws pieces
into a sack, stuffs molecules
up its sleeve for later.
He who steals from himself, steals trash.

Bone marrow breaking down is orderly
like a factory, the mind unaware.
Everything softens.
This is specific:
a swelled stomach is malnutrition;
a mind going first, starvation.
The body is eating its ponderous morsel,
holding itself tighter,
urging this slow normality,
this last flesh.
Food now kills quicker than poison.

The body bullies the lungs into push-ups,
tells the heart, "You're next."
Loudly, it brags to the door of the spirit.
At last finds rebellion.
Here, the spirit is feasting.
The spirit pounds on the door of the body
and will not go away.

River of No Return

In truth, it was a mushy movie
with Monroe and Mitchum.
It was about . . . love.
We wanted something to rush over us
and take us without thinking.
We wanted something.

Years later, I saw it, while
riding by on a city bus.
The creek that ran under the highway
displayed two events on its sloped marquee.
On one side of the river was
a flowing, pink nightgown.
You had to wonder how it got there,
someone dreaming too hard, a spirit
lying down, then forgetting to dress.
This could be about love, a rendezvous
swim, the lovers waking up safe
in different beds,
one without her gown.

On the other side of the river,
a woman's body with no shoes
was lying enchanted near the water.
She was what they were now screaming about,
her body pale enough to be that spirit,
sleepless lover, as if white light
from an old movie shone on her face.

Faye Kicknosway was born in Detroit in 1936. Her latest book is *All These Voices, New and Selected Poems.* She is currently the Visiting Writer at the University of Hawaii.

Photo by Pat Matsueda

Breath

When a man gets very old, he gets very thin, and if he's not watched closely, each breath leaving him will carry with it, concealed in its pockets or in the lining of its coat, small pieces of his internal organs and, finally, the insides of his veins and arteries. The man will grow pale as moss agate, and his skin will actually look milky the way the stone does, with tiny black outlines like winter trees, which is his breath standing above him. If one cannot catch his breath by the shoulder and shake the small packages of meat it hides in its arms back into the nose of the old man, the old man will become transparent as a lung and wheeze and, with the sound, break apart, his very skin stolen and slipped down the pants leg of his breath as it runs, escaping out the window. There will be no corpse, not even an indentation in the bed where the old man had lain, dying. Not even his sweat will be left.

Woman

There is a woman standing in the doorway. She has sallow skin and hair like metal shavings. Her dress fits her as though it had been dropped onto her from the ceiling. She is fatigued and would like to sit down, but there is only one chair in the room she faces and it is pulled up to a table and the sleeper is bent forward, his arms folded upon the table and his head rested upon his arms. There is a window near the table, and the curtain blows out from it, touching the fingers of the hand nearest it. It is raining. There is no fragrance in the rain, no scent which is clear and distinguishable. The woman in the doorway touches her face, remembering how as a girl she liked to walk in the rain with her head turned up into it, her fleshy tongue escaped and protuberant between her open lips, catching the rain into her mouth.

When Speech Comes

I

If you could have played the piano, or danced, or learned to put your face in the water, or stayed thin, or gotten taller, had a tongue full of language to enthrall any audience you wished to enthrall, if you had never listened to your mother's advice, had run away when you had money, gone traveling where you wanted to go, listened to music more up-to-date, been an only child, loved sending postcards, laughing, wiggling, if you had exercised your whims, had thrown more fits, stayed awake longer, owned your own bicycle, helped more with the chores around the house, sang out loud, been filled with longing to know the names of all the plants growing in the yard, you would not be so unhappy now.

II

Wicked, wicked girl, hair unkempt, a rat's nest, a mealie pie, no ribbons in it, no comb come near it; why, why, where is her reason? His nose avows she has not washed, and her dress, all spittled down, frumpy girl—he has no heart to scold her. Half-grinning, she holds on to the table edge with one hand and with the other hand reaches up to scratch his beard.

III

My pretty blossom, my tiny foot, my welcoming pasture, little goat, how contented I am to be near you, to hear you sweat, feel you snore, such a long time separated, no longer so no longer, my arbor, my vine, my most pretty little room, all scrubbed, so neatly cleaned, so perfectly fitted to me, my opening expectant one, my drink so cool on my skin.

IV

You could boil her like an egg. Drag her across the yard as if she were one of her own dolls. You could feed her to the dust behind the chair. Lose her in the clock. Dissolve her as if she were toothpaste in water running down the bathroom drain. She was birthdays swallowed whole by relatives The old-time shroud, torn open, crows looking out of her. What made noise near her she grabbed in both hands and gave to her father. He was tiny, sat rocking by the frontroom window. She uncoiled him, poured the noise from her hands down his scaly back, watching how it soaked into the openings between the raised and pointy plates.

Inheritance

They made Grandpa drunk
his laughter mixed
with other noises

They bound him
carried him to the meat house

where they cut
his feet off
and pierced his legs
with wires

There were ropes
hanging down
from a rafter
and they tied
the wires to his legs
pulled him up

They slit his throat
catching his blood
in a bowl

To steady him
they braced him
with lumber
and split his breastbone
with a small ax
and cut him open

They gutted him
separating his heart
and liver
from the organs
tamping up the blood
with dry rags
to keep his taste sweet

They flailed
and quartered him

put the meat
to soak in water

They pegged his skin
to the ground
and scraped it clean

They cut the meat
into small pieces
removing the bones

Some of it
was cooked
and stuffed into bags
of cherry
and grape leaves

Other of it
was cut up small
enough to fit
into pint jars

and was pickled
after it had been rubbed
with white vinegar
white pepper
and the oils
of cinnamon
and clove

Stephen Leggett (b. 1949) has published four books of poems, the most recent being *The All-Forest* in 1980. Married, with two sons, he currently makes his home in Ann Arbor.

Photo by Steve McKay

Free Will

The world has no intent. Things break,
wear down. You can't live forever.

There is no free will. A few choices, perhaps,
given weight only by the need to make them.

The cricket in the garden has a jazz
sax soul. His song kicks, bites and spits.

He's nasty as hell but his song
is sure. Sing to a moon that will fall.

In the Rains

The rain fell heavy on our
fearlessness, and the frost fell,

and the summer died as suddenly,
bearing away the broadwings,

emptying the bamboo. *Come
poison, poison* the wind sang.

& the village turned sour,
& the daughters turned from the sons.

Japh's Oranges

It is a week past
Christmas, and into
a new year, and Japh
brings me an orange.
This one has seeds,
fish-pale in membrane,
appearing at first
as shadow in a kind
of contained ocean.
Four, five, six, they
drop into a green bowl
on the table. We both
think it is a little
funny. The day emerges so.
It is hard to explain
what it is like to love
a child growing this way—
a day here, a day there.
What we have is never
what we keep. But even so,
these weekend oranges
have a kind of temporal
grace to them. They form
the day sweet and sharp
and clear, these oranges.

So It Is
for Keith Taylor

It is possible to make anything
of anything. So it is in the world,
when so much empties into the form
of so much else, until all the ends
of all the days are tangled one
across the other in an eternal passing
of the sun, and this day, this
red *one* is a note to sound by,
and on this day I saw the simplest
bittern split the sky above the marsh,
and saw it land, one reedy leg
one way, the other, the other way,
as if the ends of the earth were met,
and the bittern dropped from the world
into the underworld beneath the world,
and froze into stillness, beyond the rim,
uttering its cry, which made me think then
the whole universe was clearing its throat.

Galesburg

Carl Sandburg was born here,
just a few feet from these tracks,
in a tiny house—how
large our houses have grown!—
our most democratic poet,
a railman's son, I wish
I could have shaken his
hand, I really do. So careless
with structure, formless
and rambling, he stayed with one
woman all his life, that
Steichen girl, Paula, and together
they're buried here, side
by side, in a garden filling
with leaves. To live one
life along one seam,
to know the beginning runs
all the way to the end, un-
broken, the way people never
do anymore. . . . I see my son only
on weekends, my poems are
seldom and spare, I left
the only place I could ever
know, and never knew it, somehow
years ago my life leaped
the tracks and now goes on
side by side with this one—
But I've been to Chicago, too,
and if I have to be delivered
a hundred times in a hundred
towns to make just this one
life go through, damn it, Carl, I will.

The Form It Takes

I had almost lost the will to sing,
or any faith in the form it takes,
when I lifted an old board in the woodshed,
and found the earthbound side
covered with snail shells.

I thought of you, semblance,
growing into your life, and my own,
with a sureness that astonishes. These
shells astonish.

Lives form inside these clinging
cabinets, awash on the lifted face
of the earth. What they leave behind is beautiful.

A simple steady faith moves across
the whole plank of existence, and no snail
is ever anything else in its
stillness. The shell is not grown
into but *out of*, like a life.

Philip Legler (b. 1928) lives in Marquette and is the author of three collections of poetry, *A Change of View, The Intruder,* and his new book of Upper Penninsula poems, *North Country Images.*

Photo by Lillian Heldreth

The Survivor

It was there all along, your nightmare,
like a body lost to the lake,
swept under like a child
and never given a burial.
Jim, could you feel the undertow
where the current took your father,
washed up, down in the basement,
the shotgun handed to you years after?

In the family stories you've told
it was there all along by its absence—
love, preserved at that depth,
has kept things in their place
like photographs to come home to.

No wonder, the other night,
you sweat in your sleep
when the lake washed him up to your door,
beaching him like a fish.
Why shouldn't you throw him back,
slamming the door in his face?
Today's paper does not report
a storm on the lake, a person found.

Philip Legler

The Way Back

Canada geese wedge over
our town, lifting, spreading
a V, finding their way
back. Leaves go yellow
and red, flare for a moment
before they fall. Geese circle,
trail, speckle the sky,
leaving a mark on our minds
like your jet trail. Banking
over the bay, they turn
now into their lanes.

So, too, you were flown back
who would have driven home
to Newfield, in New York,
saving your money. Now,
not fussing in your seat,
not fidgeting about the trip
or frowning into your days,
you go, without goodbyes.
We can imagine your flight
over the pines, the great lake,
leaving us all, at last,
the way the geese disappear.

We see you, stooped, out back,
checking the rows, your garden
now weeds. When winter comes
and snow falls, burying the yard,
we'll think of geese rising,
taking the flyway back,
and your plane in morning light
climbing, breaking away.

An Old Home Movie

Here's the picture. I'm there raking leaves,
making a face. See me scattering the leaves,
dancing a jig, packing them, twisting, tying
the bags, a glimpse of coming attractions.
And those other signs, the cedar shrubs
tied, storm windows set in, windbreakers
and gloves, a preview. Your attention please:
two bikes we wheel to the basement. Notice
that look on my face, as if those Indian summer
days might be ahead. I want to slow down, slam
the brakes on the season, waddle backwards,
Charlie Chaplin retracing his steps. When the bags
untie themselves, stand, breathe open like three
wishes, the leaves rise and sail to their branch,
flare, go green against the coming snow's falling.

Eggs
for Mrs. Chinn's 5th Grade Class,
Phelps School, Ishpeming, Michigan

It was delivered, all right,
like a secret message,
the way, when I was a boy,
the milkman arrived,
as if we had taken an oath
like the one I swore on
with Donald Stutson with a pin
when we sneaked out back
behind the garage, vowing we'd
run away. It was eight o'clock
and getting light out and my wife
said when she phoned me at work,
"You'll never believe it!"
So what could I do
but rush out the door
as if for the first time
seeing the snow melting.
And how could I shout it
feeling the wind off the lake
puffing my shirt out,
rattling the traffic signs.
It was kite weather.
And striding back home on Pine
I noticed the houses I passed
stood out in their roofs
with the snow off, the way
the lake rises when the ice
breaks up and you know the first
ore boat, the *Edward B. Green,*
will dock at the harbor.
Almost home, stepping home,
I was sure all the joggers
would nod or wave on their path.
I was sure the day would fill
with the sun and women
and clothes baskets.
Opening the front door,
leaving the front door open,

I ran back into the kitchen—
it was there on the table
next to the dishes, somebody's
miracle hurting my eyes,
like staring into the sun
to make myself sneeze.
The house was empty
and I was dreaming again,
cupping my hands.
But it was your card, P. S.
sending me hunting:
"In the three mixed colored ones
there is a note," you said,
as if you were smuggling
clues in like "Count ten paces
from the steps to the maple
tree." And I reached down
into the cellophane grass
to find a trinity of eggs
and lifted them out
and opened them up
and read your words
this one good Friday to cry
what I never cried as a boy.

Thomas Lynch was born in Detroit in 1948 and has been a life-long resident of Michigan. For 15 years, he has lived and worked in Milford, where he is the funeral director. His poems have appeared in periodicals in the United States and in Ireland, including *Poetry, The Agni Review, The Midwest Quarterly, Poetry Ireland Review,* and *The Quarterly.* His first collection, *Skating with Heather Grace,* was published in 1987.

Photo by Michael Heffernan

Like My Father Waking Early

Even for an undertaker, it was odd.
My father always listened through the dark,
half-dreaming hours to a radio
that only played police and fire tunes.
Mornings, he was all the news of break-ins, hold-ups,
now and then a house gone up in flames
or a class of disorder he'd call, frowning,
a *Domestic*. They were dying in our sleep.
My father would sit with his coffee and disasters,
smoking his Luckies, reading the obits.
"I've buried boys who played with matches
or swam alone or chased balls into streets
or ate the candy that a stranger gave them . . ."
or so he told us as a form of caution.
When I grew older, the boys he buried toyed
with guns or drugs or drink or drove too fast
or ran with the wrong crowd headlong into peril.
One poor client hung himself from a basement rafter—
heartsick, as my father told it, for a girl.
By sixteen, I assisted with the bodies,
preparing them for burial in ways
that kept my dread of what had happened to them busy
with arteries and veins and chemistries—
a safe and scientific cousin, once removed
from the horror of movements they never made.
Nowadays I bury children on my own.
Last week two six-year-olds went through the ice
and bobbed up downstream where the river bends
through gravel and shallows too fast to freeze.
We have crib deaths and cancers, suicides,
deaths in fires, deaths in cars run into trees,
and now I understand my father better.
I've seen the size of graves the sexton digs
to bury futures in, to bury children.
Upstairs, my children thrive inside their sleep.
Downstairs, I'm tuning in the radio.
I do this like my father, waking early,
I have my coffee, cigarettes and worry.

Liberty

Some nights I go out and piss on the front lawn
as a form of freedom—liberty from
porcelain and plumbing and the Great Beyond
beyond the plumbing and the sewage works.
Here is the statement I am trying to make:
To say I am from a fierce bloodline of men
who made their water in the old way, under stars
that overarched the North Atlantic where
the River Shannon empties into sea.
The ex-wife used to say Why can't you pee
in concert with the most of humankind
who do their business tidily indoors?
It was gentility or envy, I suppose,
because I could do it anywhere, and do
whenever I begin to feel encumbered.
Still, there is nothing, here in the suburbs,
as dense as the darkness in West Clare
nor any equivalent to the nightlong wind
that rattles in the hedgerow of white-thorn there
on the east side of the cottage yard in Moveen.
It was a market day in Kilrush, years ago:
my great-great-grandfather bargained with tinkers
who claimed it was white-thorn that Christ's crown was made
     from,
so he gave them 2 and 6 and brought it home—
mere sapling then—as a gift for the missus,
who planted them between the house and garden.
For years now, men have slipped out the back door
during wakes or wedding feasts or nights of song
to pay their homage to the holy trees
and, looking up into that vast firmament,
consider Liberty in that last townland where
they have no crowns nor crappers, or ex-wives, either.

For the Ex-Wife on the Occasion of Her Birthday

Let me say outright that I bear you no
unusual malice anymore. Nor
do I wish for you tumors or loose stools,
blood in your urine, oozings from any orifice.
The list is endless of those ills I do not pray befall you:
night sweats, occasional itching, PMS,
fits, starts, ticks, boils, bad vibes, vaginal odors,
emotional upheavals or hormonal disorders;
green discharges, lumps, growths, nor tell-tale signs of gray;
dry heaves, hiccups, heartbreaks, fallen ovaries
nor cramps—before, during, or after. I pray you only
laughter in the face of your mortality
and freedom from the ravages of middle age:
bummers, boredom, cellulite, toxic shock and pregnancies;
migraines, glandular problems, the growth of facial hair,
sagging breasts, bladder infections, menopausal rage,
flatulence or overdoses, hot flashes or constant nausea,
uterine collapse or loss of life or limb or faith
in the face of what might seem considerable debilities.
Think of your life not as half-spent but as half-full
of possibilities. The Arts maybe, or
Music, Modern Dance, or Hard Rock Videos.
Whatever, this is to say I hereby recant
all former bitterness and proffer only all the best
in the way of Happy Birthday wishes.
I no longer want your mother committed,
your friends banished, your donkey lovers taken out and shot
or spayed or dragged behind some Chevrolet of doom.
I pray you find that space or room or whatever it is
you and your shrink have always claimed you'd need
to spread your wings and realize your insuperable potential.
Godspeed is what I say, and good credentials:
what with your background in fashions and aerobics,
you'd make a fairly bouncy brain surgeon
or well-dressed astronaut or disc jockey.
The children and I will be watching with interest
and wouldn't mind a note from time to time
to say you've overcome all obstacles this time;
overcome your own half-hearted upbringing,
a skimpy wardrobe, your lowly self-esteem,

the oppression of women and dismal horoscopes;
overcome an overly dependent personality,
stretch marks, self-doubt, a bad appendix scar,
the best years of your life misspent on wifing and mothering.
So let us know exactly how you are once
you have triumphed, after all. Poised and ready
on the brink of, shall we say, your middle years,
send word when you have gained by luck of the draw,
the kindness of strangers, or by dint of will itself
if not great fame then self-sufficiency.
Really, now that I've my hard-won riddance of you
signed and sealed and cooling on the books against
your banks and creditors; now that I no
longer need endure your whining discontent,
your daylong, nightlong carping over lost youth,
bum luck, spilt milk, what you might have been,
or pining not so quietly for a new life in
New York with new men; now that I have been
more or less officially relieved of
all those hapless duties husbanding
a woman of your disenchantments came to be,
I bid you No Deposits, No Returns,
but otherwise a very Happy Birthday.
And while this mayn't sound exactly like good will
in some important ways it could be worse.
The ancients in my family had a way with words
and overzealous habits of revenge
whereby the likes of you were turned to birds
and made to nest among the mounds of dung
that rose up in the wake of cattle herds
grazing their way across those bygone parishes
where all that ever came with age was wisdom.

Naomi Long Madgett (b. 1923) lived in Virginia, New Jersey, Missouri, and New York before coming to Michigan. She has lived in Detroit since 1946. Her six collections of poetry include *Star by Star, Pink Ladies in the Afternoon,* and *Exits and Entrances,* and her work has been widely anthologized. She is professor emeritus at Eastern Michigan University and is a 1987 recipient of a Creative Artist award from the Michigan Council for the Arts.

City Nights
for Gertrude and Eddie

My windows and doors are barred
against the intrusion of thieves.
The neighbors' dogs howl in pain
at the screech of sirens.
There is nothing you can tell me
about the city
I do not know.

On the front porch it is cool and quiet
after the high-pitched panic passes.
The windows across the street gleam
in the dark.
There is a faint suggestion of moon-shadow
above the golden street light.
The grandchildren are asleep upstairs
and we are happy for their presence.

The conversation comes around to Grampa Henry
thrown into the Detroit River by an Indian woman
seeking to save him from the sinking ship.
(Or was he the one who was the African prince
employed to oversee the chained slave-cargo,
preventing their rebellion, and for reward
set free?)
The family will never settle it; somebody lost
the history they had so carefully preserved.

Insurance rates are soaring.
It is not safe to walk the streets at night.
The news reports keep telling us the things
they need to say: The case
is hopeless.

But the front porch is cool and quiet.
The neighbors are dark and warm.
The grandchildren are upstairs dreaming
and we are happy for their presence.

Black Poet
(In memory of Langston Hughes)

How we are nourished by
his every word!
How we roll it around
in our mouths
like ripe fruit
wishing to savor it long,
digest it slowly
into our selves!

He has cut down our harps
from drooping willows
and handed them back to us
commanding us to sing.
Our blues voices
he has amplified into
anthems of praise,

gathered fragments
of our splintered dreams,
kneaded them together
in healing hands and cried,
"Be whole!"

Surely it is his
nimble fingers still
that teach us how
to harvest ripe figs
from thorn trees
that were supposed to die.

Jogging at the Health Club

In mirrors reflected in mirrors
I meet myself coming and going,
I leave by the same doors I enter,
the rooms I inhabit instantly vanish.

Through doubled eyes I watch my face dividing,
colliding with itself: splintered
selves casting many-colored prisms
in all directions at once, folding
into themselves, reappearing,
devouring, multiplying . . .

On such a runway do I recognize
refractions of my self, accepting
that all things are divisible, that
one's sum of parts is other
than a whole.

No Choice

All that I want of you I take
It's not your privilege to offer or withhold

The sun climbs the morning and has no say
in who receives its benediction

Rain falls and can't select
who is to be refreshed

You are   I take from you
all that I need

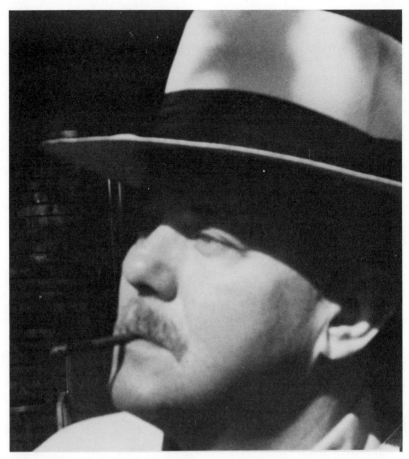

Hank Malone (b. 1941) was born in Detroit, grew up in Seattle, Washington, and returned to Detroit to complete his formal education. He is a psychotherapist with his own private practice, and he has published two books of poems and four chapbooks. His latest book, *Survival, Evasion, and Escape,* was nominated in 1986 for a Pushcart Prize, and he has received awards from the National Endowment for the Arts and the Academy of American Poets.

Chicken

my taste for
crispy spicy chicken
has bounced me around town
lately.

especially to one
take-out
where the waitress
is full of magic, hot sauce

& great love handles.
her body
is a moving darkness
that fires like a rimshot when i walk in.

i think we're in love—
staring at each other, smiling in overbites
through the 4 inch thick plexiglass
zoo-&-riot architecture.

i'm the only white guy
i've ever seen in the place.
most of the time i'm tired
& hungry when i swing through the door.

& she's always ready.
something tells me that if
there weren't so much plexiglass
& race & social grace

that we'd be married by now,
& kissing a lot & laughing in bed.
as it works, the best we can do—
well, she slips me extra jalapeno peppers

& free glasses that don't come with my order,
& i stare at her, & tilt my hat & wink
& i really give her everything, including $7.28.

i suppose she does this with other guys, too.

Trains in Detroit

Of all the songs I've heard of trains
none has sung to ghost-throated city trains
that stand around like bums on tracks, breathing and shifting,
dozing in the grey snow, in heavy coats of muddy soot.

No song yet dreamt for those blue-bloated louts
that move splintering steel a few city blocks, and return,
heaving in shivering thunder to stand the same again, hooting
and flashing out with great whorish wails!

Of all those songs I've heard about the trains
they've all been steaming streaks along the countryside,
    whistling
to some folksinger's beck and call. But let me hear a song for
    deadly toil,
for city trains; for reluctant things, overloaded, standing in the
    snow.

The Rich

The rich don't need to hear anything you say.
The boredom of their faces, rising like patient steam,
is nothing but pure blindness to your soul.

What could you possibly say to an aristocrat
who has been so rich for thirty generations?
What words mustered as their huge yachts loom into dock?

You may scream like a choirboy that history will defeat them
but their perfect gaze, perfect grooming, will echo
they have always survived your silly dreams of history.

The rich have learned how to live, and how to die,
and they have arranged this very well. And you,
you have only made an art of being loud between the two.

My Cat

I wish you could see my cat.
I don't have a cat. I have a parrot.
But I don't want you to see him.
He's a yellow featherball of noisy gibberish.

He's primitive, that's what I like about the parrot.
There's no taming him. He's like the worst
possible backalley whore you can imagine.
My jungle-jimbo turns his jail cell into paradise, singing like
    Caruso!

Better you should see my cat that doesn't exist.
Anybody can conjure one up. Imagine some Van Gogh cat—
missing an ear, an orange and bleary-eyed genius. Get my point?
It's tough to help you see this stereo-blasting Brazilian squawker,

a parrot that wants to sit and talk quietly over drinks
until it decides to crap on your hand as it screams
like some mutilated god and then stops, dead quiet, to stare
at you like an ex-wife, like an IRS agent.

Sam Spade, Therapist

She walked into my office like a single mauve glove,
ready to pay, pay hard with her heart
for my ear, for my reflex, for that white carnation
of support in my attentive eyes.

Blonde, slim, and forty-six; a sex-crazer once,
skin tight now, with too much sun-lit tennis,
too much bikini-tan, expensive booze.
She overflows, she pours me a bourbon-glass full of years.

Legs crossed well, she sat like a knicknack, in a woman's first
wintercold twilight, touching her own mortality;
her body, her blue eyes, her breasts, they could
just no longer dependably shove around her men.

Where that deep bank-account of other's lusts had been,
in the curve of leg, and throat—now
there was only tough cash, that green and familiar mold
that grew deep around a golden aging gravel-throated soul.

Money and lawyers and talk of divorce,
hours of property-talk, and the grief-talk about the kids.
The best I could do was to mop up her tears,
help to harden the heart, prepare for the ice-age,

create plans that were sane and hellish and aggressive,
like stashing the jewelry in deposit boxes and changing the
     accounts.
What a pot-boiler, and what a journey! To help steel the heart
of such a fading beauty; to sit there

in those tough sad flurries, only to help sock out the lights.

Joseph Matuzak (b. 1955) was born and raised in Flint, Michigan, and has worked a variety of jobs, from police officer trainee to vending machine stuffer to bookstore clerk to blood bank attendant. He currently manages a computer software store and writes art reviews and features for the *Flint Journal*. His work has appeared in *Kansas Quarterly, Fedora, Cedar Rock, Corridors, Passages North, Pteranadon,* and in the anthologies *Songs from Unsung Worlds, Anthology of Magazine Verse,* and *Industrial Strength Poetry.*

Photo by KEVA

The Loss of Teeth in Dreams

They are hurrying out of my mouth
in busloads, parting the red sea

of the lips on their journey
to whiter pastures. My children,

you have become so many, and I
so old, so quickly. Night to me

means suddenly I am all gums,
soft pulp against the stiffness

of the dark, my dreams
of petrified words,

clacking in hopeless order
around my tongue, nuance gone,

only the taste of the surface left.
The molar of this story is unclear,

close friends overlooked, or something,
thrice daily more habit

than devotion, a neglect of history.
How can I dream you back into place,

oh Israel, oh tooth, I need your walls against
the food of the world, that protein charge.

When life puts its hand to my mouth
I want to leave it with your mark.

Joseph Matuzak

Tattoo

It is not a ship, or a rose, or some dullard heart
with a name for a face and an arrow through the brain.

It is an obscure literary reference,
a picture summoned up from what should have been a past,

storied relatives from thick Polish stock,
the lightning escape from another winter's boot.

This tattoo will baffle the onlookers—
"ce n'est pas grave, he was drunk when it was done,

I'm sure it can be removed or the punch line drawn in."
On this arm is the professor's masterwork;

Berryman decoded and rendered in an art deco motif,
and somewhere on the buttock a portrait of Pound.

If you love language, you must let it get under your skin,
or maybe the other way around. It's all a matter

of ink, I say to the king of needles,
and he nods, and pricks in another footnote.

Porno

When I say love I mean legs like garage doors,
skin like pumice, a voice that speaks only the ache

that is my name. I see you, rich and glossy, high-contrast,
the mole on your belly shining, a fixed star

above an ever trembling, ever hungry land.
In my hands, the pages of your body writhe and grind,

quick as film, silvery and warm. I am made completely
of nerve endings, a drawing by Vesalius,

a million tiny cords topped by eyes waiting for your touch.
With you I whisper the language of closeness,

of largeness: act meaning actual, want meaning wanton,
love meaning anyone and no one at all.

The Runners

Always, Coach tells us, there is someone
who can twist a little tighter before the snap,

the sound of time cracking, or distance, a crowd roar,
long hymen of tape tearing across the chest.

In the desert you learn the ground will not bear
your weight, sand like foam in a mixing bowl.

Coach preaches keeping light, like birds do,
hollow bones winging weight at the clouds,

no footprints, that old Indian trick, our motto.
We practice every day, hot, playing tag with mirages,

you're it, and faces in those wavy pictures
bounced here from far cities look surprised.

He told us running would harden our legs, would marble
our muscles until we were Greek statues, cold and ready,

the very portraits of speed. And then he smiled,
said forget all that, just run, try to catch something.

A man in town for the New York City Marathon
met three thugs who pistol-whipped him, slicing

from jaw to temple, and stripped his watch and wallet.
He raced anyway, pretended each man ahead was an attacker,

tapping them so gently with bandaged fingers as he sped by
that some stopped in confusion, the light touch like a charm,

whispering, you, too, are beaten. Lay your hand,
says Coach, on the air like that. Make it gasp.

Ash

I pick a teacup so long unused that dust clings
inside like paint, to be cooked and bullied clean.

The tea leaves surrender their own bitter dirt,
water leaching, coaxing clear the true strong color,

the way autumn leaves cry out, strangled, before they fall.
I think my own color ripens ever closer, now, to the surface,

wary of the rain that swells the old window casings
tightly shut, heating the air trapped within.

And I think of the way the earth gripped my shoes
as I tramped across the cemetery on my lunch hour

like through a corridor at school, classrooms
and teachers in neat exclamatory rows beside me.

It had been too long, father; I did not
find your stone, did not really think I would.

But I remembered the way the young priest,
heart full of God and goodness, poured his sacrament

over you, calling you already by the wrong name.
I thought of the ends of your Camel cigarettes,

how they riveted me as a child; the glory
of fire, hard, magically hewing whatever it touched

into another shape, ash, the skeleton of dirt,
bone left after the flame burns low. When I am gone,

when my brothers and sisters are as well,
you will be forgotten by all but the earth,

because you were only a good man.
Already you are myth, a belief in a dark forest,

a cover like gold leaf which ornaments my life.
It is the same for me, I know, and this is why

what I remember most was the moist breeze
that followed me as I returned to my workaday life—

a hand raising itself like a delicate cup to my lips,
warming anything I might offer as a goodbye.

Judith Minty was born, raised, educated, and married, and raised a family in Michigan. Her first book, *Lake Songs and Other Fears*, received the United States Award of the International Poetry Forum. Her other books include *Yellow Dog Journal, Letters to My Daughters, In the Presence of Mothers,* and *Counting the Losses.* She presently lives in New Era, Michigan, and Trinidad, California.

Photo by Scott Ryan

Destroying the Cormorant Eggs

Black, black as the plumage
of the Double-crested Cormorant, all black
except for the orange chin pouch below its slender,
curved bill, who nests along the shore in shadow and crack
of rock along with the lighter, tan or gray or white
gulls and terns on Little Gull Island and Gravelly Island
in the middle of Lake Michigan— Black as the long shadow
of this fisherman, or madman, slipping
over these rocks, these nests, an eclipse or is it God,
some thing without conscience between sun and earth/water,
his staff much like a shepherd's crook, but
this time carried for balance and for the rest of it: the
choosing, knowing which eggs, only lovely pale blue,
not the gull's and tern's brown or buff, then
to lift out, hurl against the granite,
to punish them for fishing these waters,
to crush under boot or beat with his stick,
2000 eggs, the silent cormorants now emitting faint squawks,
flapping their black wings over this darkness,
the albumin and yolk, the embryos shining on dull rock,
the small pieces of sky fallen down— Black
as the night waters of a man's dream where he gropes
below the surface, groaning with the old hungers,
the luminescence of his skin now covered by something
so thick his arms stroke heavy with it, the water
without end, and no island, no island in sight.

Judith Minty

Walking the Beach in Fog

In this blind world, lost
between sunrise and evening, the dog and I
follow the shoreline north.
No tourists will come here today.
The dunes have disappeared and the horizon,
the sky, the driftwood logs and ore boats.
We exist in only a circle of light.
The dog stays within range of my voice—
we don't want to lose each other—
muted, without color, we're dots
on a fractured piece of landscape
where even the water has lost all blue:
If we were a painting, we'd be
"black dog and woman in white," nameless,
suspended, viewed by no one, walking nowhere.
Ahead and behind swirls another world and I think
of that winter I skied in Switzerland
when we were caught in clouds coming down the mountain,
when I was young, when I lost
my sense of up and down and thought I was floating.
We groped our way then, cautious ghosts
traversing the trail. With each turn on the descent,
we had to bend low, touch the snow, make sure
it was under us. Today there's just the dog and me,
whatever waits ahead remains unseen.
Even these deer tracks fade to nothing. If I
walk deeper into this fog, the dog may not follow me
and if she doesn't, what will know me there?

Celebrating the Mass

In this hospital room, lacking the hands
of a nurse, I braid my daughter's hair
into corn-rows. She is nineteen now.
When did I stop touching my child?
We have eaten sandwiches brought in and picked
at food on her tray, then turned to the mirror.
Helpless in these weeks of testing, waiting,
we want to alter her life in some way.

I think of those other mothers who have done this,
their backs aching, their hands tightening.
I think of them standing long hours
on porches of farm shacks maybe, or in tenement rooms.
I think of them weaving dark strands
to make their daughters beautiful
after the meals were served, after
the mending, the washing hung, the fields hoed.

Here, a comb sets our boundaries.
Fingers separate and part, we begin
another row: blond hair lifted, pulled,
the pattern worked in. I sculpt to the shape of bone.
Now six braids done. Now an hour. Now nineteen years.
We learn each other again. Hands to head,
fingers knitting a cap, we begin
at the temple, around the ear, crown to nape.

A Sense of Place

I.

I recall that California yard full of caged birds
we used to drive past on our way to the ocean
and the parrot shop at the Santa Cruz Mall, alive
with exotic feathers—we all dressed in colors then—
that woman in the red cape who wandered mission Blvd.,
street musicians in Guatemalan shirts,
flower shops with tubs of roses by the curb.
Now I'm in snow country, still thinking
of pink and yellow buildings, of persimmons
in the market, and rhododendrons flopping off their stems.
Here, these Eastern woods have just shrugged off winter
and the trees are full of brown birds,
bright voices hiding in the branches.

II.

Summers ago in Leland, I watched a swimmer
walk out of Lake Michigan, her wet hair gleaming
and her skin, with its coat of oil,
glittering in the sun. Behind her, blue
and stretching to the sky, the water sparkled.
Everything shone, even crystals of sand around our blanket.
That was the month of butterflies, thousands
of monarchs on their way to Mexico—
I don't know how they can make it so far.
Once, in California, I walked
through the eucalyptus trees at night
and heard the whisper of their wings while they slept.

III.

When the bear came to me, I already knew
that trees walk at night, that the river speaks
and the wind knows everything.

It was October, evening at the Yellow Dog. I was
reading near the stove, trying to keep warm, trying
to ignore some mice building a nest on the shelf.
Maybe he was watching all week, maybe
he just saw my light—I don't know.
At first I thought his bawling and crying
were embers in the stove, then a cow,
but those Michigan woods were never farmland.
I turned down the lamp and ran to the window, but there was
only my own reflection in the light from the fire.

IV.

Just weeks ago I sat on the bank
of the Smith River, up near the Oregon border.
I was mourning snow then, dreaming white hills
and wishing cold wind in the face.
Now, I'm across the country and ice
has just let loose this pond. It's May,
bass shiver up from the mud and new leaves
reflect on the water's skin. I feel lucky
they've found me, whoever they are
that flow with the water, float on the wind.
At this moment, now, midges and darters skim the surface
and the bass break in circles to take them.

(Saratoga Springs, NY)

Ben Mitchell (b. 1952), a native West Virginian now living in southwestern Michigan, is the Fine Arts Editor of *Passages North* and director of the *Dance Center Exhibit Series*, the art gallery of Kalamazoo's Wellspring Dance Collaborative. His poems have appeared in *Prism International, Montana Review, Grand Valley Review, Mississippi Mud*, and *Great River Review*. He recently received fellowships from the Millay Colony for the Arts and Virginia Center for the Creative Arts.

Photo by David Kamm

Revolutionary Piano
Joseph Beuys, 1969

All over the cluttered keyboard, the usual configurations of
    beauty.
Hung on the wall behind him framed in mitered wood:
Pastel landscapes, carefully drawn crystals of salt
crusted around the ankles of tourists,

grave photographs of Japanese monks caught stiffly raking their
    sand.
In the distance, beyond the windows grey and filmy with tobacco
    smoke,
pigeons and mourning doves float, suspended miraculously
over Berlin like rain, a rain which hums
itself to sleep inside the walls at night. From
somewhere inside the piano the recorded sounds of reindeer
pawing frozen tundra. Everything wrapped

in raw felt. Honeysuckle is far away. A glass case
around the piano, stems of roses wrapped in the strings,
sewn over the pedals, dampening the expected, potential music.
And lying there on the octave above middle C
like a slum in this civilization of logic and invention
under the unmistakable, harsh red of roses
is a rabbit that is no longer rabbit or even *animal*.

The small body of its side in a litter of splinters
where a bone was shaved. Don't let anyone ever tell you
the revolutionary piano does not make memorable music.
I've heard it said the rabbit cries out
only once at the moment of its death,
a pitiful, ash-thick terrifying sound, after
its quick life spent in silence.
It's not true, this animal's forgotten throat is full.

Somewhere the Letter O Makes a Sound We Least Expect to Hear

In this play something is lost. I watched light fiddle all day on the laurel, mud harden and preen its wrinkles in the sun. Or: watched the young dwarf walk painfully across the backyard, and when he reached the fence . . .
What do you think he did next?

Nothing is taken for granted. I am writing a play about a woman who would not speak. This has been going on for years. The speeches I've written for her are useless, as if her feelings were imaginary, a one-lane bridge. Where she sits stroking her thighs with tobacco-stained hands, she watches me. Reading grandfather's letters again, remembering the leg they cut off his son. History's like that, misplaced parts. From my chair I smell her cheap perfume spread below her throat, so voice and speech are believable, the appetite for understanding. Emptiness. I'm writing a play about a woman who lived alone in a boarding house and would not speak.

I am writing a play in which light and sound and the smell of a few old men is nothing believable, nothing like desire for sound, nothing like the desire for emptiness. Our knowledge of this world, like grief, incomplete.
These are the parts.

Conscience

I almost never think about it. Admit that it's difficult to feel at
home. And there's the sexual sound of water, a stone dropped
there. Crouched just off the road, a car's headlights pass and
you're caught holding the charred telephone, the monkey skull,
motel keys. Later, repeat the story over drinks so someone's wife
is shocked and justifiably intrigued, and lying as we do tell of
running all night, tell of the road, that you had no choice but to
begin it all again. Pausing long enough to watch through
theatrically half-closed eyes her breasts lifting and settling under
white cotton, satisfied, finish, leaving out the orphans. The long
night. Carrying everything I loved from the edge of the woods to
its dim, fortunate interior, cleaning the rusted shovel, settling
against a tree to smoke, denying nothing, trying to fill in with
precision that sense of helplessness, the possible, utter beauty of
destruction.

Husband, Wife, Fish

Once there was a kind man who loved his life very much. So much
he didn't wish for anything. He was a fisherman, like the rest of
us, and loved the sucking noise the sea made at his feet, the scar
the line cut through the water, the line humming with moisture
and fish. You know the story, he caught one that offered anything
imaginable. There is the emptiness in this story. But, wanting
nothing, he dragged all his wife's desire down there for the greedy
magic. Each time he asked for more the sea changed color. Black
at the end of the story, and they returned to the small hut where
they'd begun, rotten nets on the porch, broken boat in the yard,
nothing like the laughter or grief of children. Let's say the man got
wise, went on the sly to visit the fish again, many years later, says,
Listen, I've changed my mind, I don't want to be god or anything,
nothing . . . I want a new wife, some children that mend when
they break themselves, a small boat without leaks to take them out
in, stories to tell as their eyes flutter closed. The fish is angry, turns
the sea to ink again, flings from the bottom all the debris and bones
that fester there, so the fisherman's buried under a mountain of
garbage. It's an old story. Later, after the fish has gone, a small
child crawls out of the pile, a small child covered with slime and
slick wrinkled purple skin, picks up the old fisherman's pole, casts
the line far out into the pure white water.

Anne Ohman-Youngs was born in 1939 in Marquette and lives in Escanaba. She is an associate editor for *Passages North* and a part-time English Instructor at Bay de Noc Community College in Escanaba. Her poetry has been published in *Ball State University Forum, Visions/BBP,* and *Tar River Poetry.*

Photo by Michael Youngs

Cutting Wood

1.

After the war
my father put away his leather flying helmet,
bought a farm and planted strawberries,
corn and potatoes, pushed his days
into the earth like seed. Each October
he walked hard fields into the woods,
dragged windfall branches to the barn.
He taught me to swing the small axe where we cut
and stacked winter heat. Those weeks before he died
he carved a bird from a knot of wood,
hung it from the mirror with twine.
Each morning his eyes caught its flight.

2.

The chain saw shrieks all afternoon,
bites firebox lengths
from eight-foot logs I feed
along the sawhorse cradle.
Sweat runs down my breasts
and I imagine my hands slipping,
fingers dropping like sawdust.
My father's axe broke large branches
with a quick, sharp sound. When finished
he buried the blade in the chopping stump
and I leaned on the handle, watched his handsaw
rush across smaller wood. Once he gave me
a can of sawdust and I fattened pincushions,
a stocking doll with brown embroidered eyes.

3.

Two weeks
and ten cords stack the shed.
I count growth rings
on the last log—twenty years,
an hour of fire. I sweep
sawdust into plastic bags,

suddenly think "pincushions"
and fill a coffee can
with sawdust. I pick up
the hand axe, split October afternoons
from kindling logs. Somewhere
my father smiles
at the smooth arc of swing,
the clean snap of each cut.

Executions

A neighbor gave my father a hen
past laying. I squatted
in the dust to watch it peck
a fistful of corn,
stroked its silky feathers
while my father sharpened the axe.

When he slid his thumb along the blade
I grabbed his arm.
He moved away, looped twine
around the hen's legs,
jerked it upside down
and hung it against a fencepost.

Before I could shut my eyes
the axe hit and the head dropped
on his boot, bounced between us
splatting blood on my bare feet,
my body so still
a fly crawled on my eyelid.

He reached to brush it away
and I hit him and ran down the path
to the garden, tore out
the heaviest tomato plants,
squashed each ripened fruit
as if it were my father's hands.

Anne Ohman-Youngs

Markers

The night I woke up
and saw my father
drown the kittens,
I packed their struggle
and all my silence
in a shoebox,
lined it with my favorite blouse.
Early morning darkness hid
the funeral by a lilac bush
in the backyard.

My son wanders
this same backyard
and finds, after all these years,
the rounded stone, the wooden ruler
I had pounded
until it marked death.
He kneels, bends his head to the ground
and listens
as if he can hear the secrets
a woman keeps.

After Placing My Father in a Nursing Home

I touch the car horn
and five crows
fly up from a rabbit,
a raccoon—road-kill.
Shoulders hunched
they clutch tree branches, wait
for passing cars and trucks.

Once a Least Shrew crossed
the living room floor, dodged
under a closet door.
Later I found it
in the bathtub, trapped
by steep sides.

I left it there
to die. Shut away
from fields and tunnels
it ran the length
and width of the tub
for an hour.

Ahead there is just the road.
So much is honorable in the rabbit,
the raccoon, the crow.

John Palen born in 1942 in Missouri, lives in
Midland and teaches journalism at Central Michigan
University. His poems have appeared recently in
*Passages North, International Poetry Review, Kansas
Quarterly,* and *Bitterroot.* His book *To Coax a Fire* was
published in 1984.

Visitation

His contempt for us was so
perfect he didn't even honk,
just whispered up on us
in his heavy, fast, mute car

going about seventy-five
down a busy, two-lane highway,
and we gave way as silently,
glided to the shoulder and felt

gravel shift beneath our tires,
only later demanding to know
"Who was that? Who the hell
was that sonofabitch?"

Volunteers

Cherry tomatoes
seeded from last year's vine tangle
sprout among the beans,
their stems well proportioned, their leaves
tightly furred. In the strip we left to grass
potato plants poke through,
like coarse, green rosebuds. Over in the onions,
cucumbers stick out their smooth green tongues.

What do we do with this inappropriate goodness,
these stragglers neither crop nor weed,
songs we can't get out of our heads
at two o'clock in the morning?

John Palen

Planting the Spinach
for LoLita and Ray

Paul writes to the Corinthians
that there is nothing love cannot face.
When did you plant spinach this year,
my neighbor asks, and since I am
normally so casual about these things
he is surprised I know. It was

the second week of March, when love faced
its own failure, and splinters of glass
seeded the snow cover. I dumped
some chicken manure in a knocked-together
cold frame and covered it with
store-bought dirt and thumbed out

seed in rows. At night before sleep
I imagined that scant, leaky haven,
the little warmth it kept. I think of it now,
looking at these veined and rooted leaves
each cupped over its own emptiness
like hands on a table of one who waits.

Dry Grass
for Fran

What's it like, you ask, to have
a friend who's a lesbian? It's like
sitting in dry grass in a meadow
on a summer's day, a half-mile

from the town's lush, watered lawns
tended only by men. I have seen them
stalking dandelions with canisters
of herbicide strapped to their shoulders

riding power mowers in methodically
tightening rectangles, near-missing
their wives' beds of phlox and marigolds.
The dry grass in the meadow is brown,

fragrant, alive, rooted in what
sustains. It is not brown in order
to be green. It keeps a vocabulary
of insects at the tip of its tongue,

repeating them over and over
into the sun. To lie back in it
is to be accepted as one is
by the natural order of things.

John Palen

Birthday

You filch the knife
from the dishwasher,
hiding it in cupped

hands like a candle.
We hear the door slam.
You're gone again

into the night you make.
Sometimes we lock you out,
sometimes not, but

you always come back.
The story repeats itself
like those fairy tales

I used to read to you,
ordeal after ordeal
varied and embellished

until the child sleeps
or the story teller tires.
Today is your birthday.

I'm gone, hundreds of miles.
No heart for it anymore,
no plans to call. No gifts.

It Won't Last Long, We Thought,

this pitcher glazed with bright
naive fish, chasing each other
to breed or devour. It was no grecian urn
but a cheap Italian import
extracted in some sweatshop
from the last of a line of potters.

I bought it at Woolworth's
for our second wedding anniversary,
that year of anger and birth.
Somehow I presented it
without demeaning you. You laid aside
your petulance to murmur thanks.

Now its rim is chipped
from a thousand usings. We've poured
from it, mixed in it, washed it
for twenty unbroken years. The fish,
forgiving and companionable now,
swim on in their slow annealing

around this made shape of clay
that year by year appears more beautiful.

Miriam Pederson (b. 1948) grew up in Minnesota and for the past ten years has lived in Grand Rapids. She has served as the coordinator for the Writers' Center, a project of the Urban Institute for Contemporary Arts. Her work has appeared in *Milkweed Chronicle, Green River Review, Passages North,* and *Woman Poet: The Midwest.* She is a part-time instructor of English at Aquinas College in Grand Rapids and conducts poetry workshops in local elementary schools for the Arts Council of Greater Grand Rapids and the Michigan Council for the Arts.

Ice Fishing

In each small shack
a man
drops a line
through a hole in the ice.
Sometimes he opens his thermos,
but mostly he waits,
tempting the casserole of walleyes.
A story passed
among the fishermen
says a dog
slipped through
a hole,
nosed its way
to the opening
in a neighboring shack.
The dog, half frozen,
split the drowsy silence,
its black head filling the space,
ears lifting like gills.
Dazed, the fisherman
probed at the creature,
and knew it was a dog
when fangs lit the dark rectangle
and widened
into shivering fur.
The man wrapped the dog
in a blanket
and headed for town.
Behind his pick-up
the waiting goes on—
a bobber jerks,
a fish fights the air,
a man removes the hook,
drops back the line
all in a motion.
He dredges the water
the winter long

caring little for the catch,
lost in a whirlpool
of hunches and dreams—
fish-dogs, mermaids, leviathans.

Interlude

There is a time before snow
when a weariness takes hold.
Lovers too tired to woo
sleep cold
in the comfortless stretch of night.

In the lull of passion
heart beats quicken
only with the drag of the rake.
The body drifts from place to place
looking for the storm windows.

When snow sticks for the first time,
whiteness stuns the lovers
from their sleep.
They fling the blankets
to the floor
and make the windows steam.

Miriam Pederson

House

The tenants switch on lights
long before dark.
Their small rooms
lean together
and the eavesdropping begins.
In number one
the tap turns on and off.
In three the fry pan spurts.
The bed creaks in six.
The manager smokes in two
wishing away the tenants
and their noise.
   He sees the house whole;
   its banisters
   guiding the family
   down for their meals,
   up for their beds.
   Shades of carpets and draperies
   deepen with the hours
   and fires are lit.
   In the library
   he passes his finger over volumes
   in the flickering light,
   rings the maid for his brandy.
Smoke curls through the room
with no place to go.
He breaks a small pane
to let in air.

Small Reminders

He left the milk to sour.
It's up to her
to empty the carton
into the sink.
She traces a message
on the waxy cardboard:
"This is the way with all whiteness.
This is the way with sheets,
bones, teeth, paper, carnations.
This is the way with socks
going about their business
behind my back.
They return
not so white, empty,
skins discarded on the bedroom floor
strange as the souring of milk."

Cups too hot to touch
steam between them
and much of what is said
rises also.
The kettle boils dry.
They didn't notice
when it stopped singing,
when quiet in the kitchen
meant parch and ruin.
They walk as if
they had stones in their shoes,
drag their feet like children
whose chores await them
at home.
From the curb
they see their shadows
lying motionless in the street.

She counts the lines
on his forehead as he sleeps.
Some furrows go deep,
others can be smoothed away.
Some years were better

than others.
In this familiar place
lit by an off-white moon
she counts and thinks of him.

Lawrence Pike was born in Detroit in 1932. He grew up in Saginaw and now lives in Royal Oak with his two sons. He teaches composition, the writing of poetry, and contemporary literature at Macomb County Community College, and is a poet in residence in the Michigan Council for the Arts Writer-in-the-Schools program. His work has appeared in *Song, Studies in Contemporary Satire, Green River Review, University of Windsor Review, The MacGuffin, Passages North,* and *5 a.m.* His books are *Now That Good Jack Armstrong's Gone* and *Hideout Matinees.* He is a past winner of the Michigan Council for the Arts Individual Artist grant.

Photo by Eric Buikema

Briggs Stadium

While Hank Greenberg was out fighting Japs,
Pete Gray, the one-armed left-fielder,
tucked his glove under his stump
before he threw to the plate
and Chuck Hostetler, sprinting & puffing,
tripped over third base in the Series.
Not that these bums weren't trying
but even Dick Wakefield's .350
went flat when Feller came back.

Well, those were the days of the rejects
who swung from the heels for a single,
who, slow-footed, dove for the grounders,
who tried for the time to be champions.
What courage! The gimps and the rookies,
they garnered a spot in the lineup—

until a returned Hankus Pankus,
his shoulders rippling like thunder,
ha! smacked the ball into the seats.

Lawrence Pike

Holiday Greetings

When zedeh Schiller gave out gelt,
silver garlic for his boy
to wave to drive away the goy—
the carols and the tree—I felt
myself and chosen tribe above
what Christian clamor had,
sure no brother Jew played God
plagiarizing laws of love.

Well, I was young and wanted lines.
And how I stayed pariah-tough!
Their sweetest Christ was not enough
to break my glass. I stood the pain,
drew from kin. Now, Jew who's grown,
who, springing outward, did not dive
into his own, who came alive
by swimming for the world around,

I've left that ghetto pool I knew.
Now I to a love confide
a song against that inbred side.
I eat a Christmas goose. Jew
who's found a new romance,
I touch new worlds. And yet I pray
to spin the dradle out of clay
and not forsake my impudence.

Embracing

We hug, you & I who've got
this chill. Sick time
leaks its mystery. We slum
our trenches late.

Once I answered to your dare
and you my call.
Genius knew itself, then spilled—
an urgent year!—

till now we hold tight terrified.
Dear God it's damp,
cold and quick. And love grows limp
and we have lied.

Services

First your tumor, then breast, then body
was gone. All we had left were grains in a bag
in a box. Then your mother and sisters, children and I
drove to the ferry and through Harsens Island
where Bert has some land he said we could use.
And your children—what order! For a few minutes
no usual yells. You should have seen them.
Your John cut the weeds, sprayed for mosquitoes.
Mikey, hair flaring from under his cap,
did most of the digging. Pete, acting on cue,
took the small fir out of his clunker,
out of his trunk, and stood at the hole
while Jess on the sidelines told Pete where to slant it,
Mike how to shovel, John when to spray,
and got no more back-talk than the warm blue spring air.
Then John took the box up to the sapling
and shook out some dust. With pieces of bone—
there still were chunks—with pieces of bone—
he salted the tree, then passed things to Jess who
tilted the box, removed the bag, let more ashes
tumble. Mikey was next. He, taking his turn,
reached in his hand, pulled out a fist-full,
then sowed more of the earth by the tree with your cells.
"Hey look! I'm the first who reached in with bare hands!"
But that is when the grabbing began. And then the yelling.
Each showed the others how to strew ashes. Then
we climbed in our cars, out of the grave. On the way home
Pete's muffler broke. Bump in the road.

John R. Reed (b. 1938) lives in Detroit and teaches English at Wayne State University. His poetry has appeared in *Paris Review, Sewanee Review, American Scholar, Ontario Review, Michigan Quarterly Review* and *Tri-Quarterly.* His book of poems *A Gallery of Spiders* was published in 1980.

Dry Earth
(Ethiopia, 1985)

A morning wind lifts the hem of dust
then gasps and lets it settle again
in lacy patterns that would be lovely
to anyone with water in a tub
or rice in a pail, but this old man,
so wrinkled he could be an incarnation
of the land, brittle and cracked everywhere,
remembers in his muscles the plow's
smooth prow cleaving the soil into black
lips like a breaking smile before him all day.

Now the hardpan clamps shut its mouth
and the land gives nothing, not even sighs.
The dream of an ox is hard within him as though
he had swallowed a stone. For many years
he lived without a need for angels.
But now he and the others and his daughter's child
—brown sticks and an empty gourd—
hunched in the gauzy shade of their tree
like ghosts, would worship any god who,
though he marked them with contempt and cursed
the land forever, would spit and make it live.

John R. Reed

A Drink of Water

Scarcely thinking, I leave my chair and saunter
to the kitchen and run the faucet until
the water's cool and fill a glass and drink.
Only then my eyes hook on the lake-blue
sky, and suddenly my mind cloudbursts back
to where I am, not under Africa's yellow
heaven heavy with dust, people scattered
like windfall fruit all around, old men thin
as forks too weak to brush away the thirsty
flies wolfing each bead of sweat, mothers
without a jangling trinket to barter for drink,
their swollen babies vainly tugging breasts
that hang down hopeless as torn pockets,
                                        while I
am where the states dangle like piglets from
the Great Lakes' swollen tits, sucking as though
their dam could never dry out like a stalk
of autumn corn. Moments ago, my mind
was elsewhere, musing that hope is the salty meat
we chew to breed our quenchless thirst for justice
or love, high thoughts I have the leisure for
because I take my water from a tap
easily as any lord may give a reprieve
while those with a different revelation suck
the dry straws of their awful clarity.

Corregio's "Io"

That look of utter absorption
in her body's pleasure,
head turned aside
to let a small cry fly
from her half-open mouth,
surprised to be taken
so heedlessly
by the violet cloud
smudging her with
its impassioned smoke.

This is the climax
of languid afternoons
when pewter skies hummed
ready for rain
and half-hearted gusts
scooted little gangs of leaves
here and there,
the unwitting dream
lazing late in bed,
the sheets sleek
and redolent as another skin,
her sumptuous breasts
nestling along her arm
like another's, her hair
trapping capricious gleams
from the smothered sun.

This is what it comes to—
an obscure god whose
surges of pleasure
so private and intense
make her eyelids shudder,
her lips part
to let the small cry
flit out and rise
like a thrush set free
into a sky of eagles.

John R. Reed

House Burning

On March 9, 1977, after years of violent
abuse, Francine Hughes burned her ex-
husband in his bed.

Carelessly you notice a blush on the gunmetal sky
then turn away to finish slicing the potatoes
or folding up old newspapers to throw away
until the sirens call you to the angry red face
of the night with its black eyebrows frowning down.

It's in the neighborhood. Another business torched
or bad connections in a house like your own.
Or a woman, crouched with her children like stuffed toys
in a crib, stares at a room's set jaw of door
where the man who drove his sex into her like a club
moments ago lies drunk. She still sees
her ravaged schoolbooks blaze and collapse into ash and mix
with the trash in their backyard barrel as though that rope
for climbing out of her fearful cave has turned to breath
and she falls to the stone floor of despair unable
to feel on her arms and face the mulled opal swellings,
the raw scrawlings of his illegible rage.

Who knows what she thinks of all the months torn
in the gears of his madness, the rasping away of every hope.
Her life is a concussion, this moment its bruise.
The gasoline's ether makes her giddy, the match snickers
its bright promise and fiery tongues whisper free
as all the night becomes one burning page.

The sirens are still. The sky cools to a common grey.
Carefully you arrange the books in your briefcase
then call to your wife who comes downstairs puzzled by the
    strange
alarm in your voice, a little surprised when you put
your arms around her and hold her face to yours,
both burning with the same unquenched desire.

Danny Rendleman (b. 1945) teaches composition and creative writing at the University of Michigan–Flint. He has published three books of poetry, and writes short stories as well. He received a Michigan Council for the Arts grant in 1986. His work has appeared in *Field, American Poetry Review, Poetry Now, Epoch,* and *Northwest Review.* He is married to the poet Jan Worth and has one son, Eliot.

Photo by Greg Brown

Getting My Father Out

The two boys out in the ambulance
are passing a joint. I can see them
through the trailer window.

They are nodding their heads
to some Twisted Sister song on the radio,
smiling, sitting out there
in the late June sun,

and I am in here to get my father out.
He is dead, so there isn't much
need to hurry, yet I wish they would.

He is in the back bedroom
beside the bed, I am out here,
they are out there. This is a still-life,
I tell myself. I look around:

an ashtray of thumbed-out Camels,
a TV Guide with Ed Asner on the cover,
my father's Romeo house-slippers
under his chair. The day is a dazzler
and I would rather be elsewhere,

on a lake, back in bed, anywhere.
But the park super called me and said,
Something's wrong, and she was right.

And now I have to tell everyone.
I'll hate that. Maybe not as much
as walking into his bedroom
and finding him on the floor staring at
infinity with his mouth open in surprise
or fear—but almost.

I mean, I got out of there, and right away—
it took two seconds, tops.
But calling all those people and telling them . . .
Aunt Agatha with her rouge and black shoes,
Uncle Florence with his . . . tubes. The rest.

That's what's so bad about death.
Not the body—hey, I can live with that—
but the phonecalls and the arrangements
and never knowing what folks will say.

I think the boys are coming now.
They're not smiling, though I can tell
they're stoned. That must be difficult, too.
They'll understand what I'm going through.

You know, I've always liked the idea of
AMBULANCE spelled backwards on the front of it:
Language meant for mirrors instead of real life.

Charlie

He expected everything. Imagine that.
On long, glowering August days
he would fathom the hard hearts
of automobiles in his garage,
insinuate his black-mooned hands
into the maze of automatic transmissions,
into the viscera of poached deer
hanging from the beams, the rain dancing
in galoshes on the corrugated steel roof above.

Half the time the customers couldn't pay,
and their cars would fill the field out back
like bodies in the rye grass and jack pine.
Half the time he would give the venison away
to Chippewa hoboes camped along the swamp.
He was my hero, skinny and bitter
in striped overalls with the knees out.

He knew things I had to know—
how to lay cement blocks for a septic tank,
twanging the plumb-line with its chalk etch
of blue, how to hammer a nail in three strokes.
How to fillet a fish and fry it
before it quite stopped wriggling.
How to drink whiskey neat in a jelly glass
all afternoon and still be able to see
a spikehorn buck along the Muskegon River
in last light and drop it to its knees
with one shot, no scope, from a hundred yards.

I didn't know any better.
I thought these were good things,
proper things for a man to know.
I was nothing like him and he knew it—
city boy who read too much,
always breaking my glasses, always
stepping on the fishing line down along
Tinny Creek where the evening brown trout
swooned under cedar logs, always complaining

about mosquitoes and blackflies and no-see-ums,
always figuring this paradise would last forever.

A GM executive owns it all now,
every outbuilding and rusted Chevy,
all the piss-poor land as far as you can walk
on a good day. Charlie died and was buried,
reeking still of gasoline and Canadian Club.
They said it was cancer of the balls and polio
doing their jobs, working overtime,
clocking him out early,
just like friends would do.

Tremor

Though the '57 Chevy my Dad
bought me was an automatic
and had four doors,
it was a hard-top with dual exhausts,
a milled cam. And mounted on that short-block
engine were two Holly four-barrel carbs.
My God, was it fast.

I heated the springs red
with a brother-in-law's stolen shop torch
until it settled just right
to cruise four inches off the ground.
I poured hot oil through
the glass-pack mufflers until,
backing down from forty in low gear,
you could hear the 283 snarling
a mile away. Or so they said.
I did this every other block.

Saturdays I would wax it all afternoon
until it glowed gold and black
and quick as a summer finch—as stark
as summer. All sweltering evening
I would wait at Walli's Drive-In
for Donald Barber to show up
in his old man's Oldsmobile.

Now I rise from your side
long past midnight some twenty-five years
later to come downstairs and write this,
as if I might ever forget it.
The dark air outside over the fields
is solid and nearly starless.
In the black and flaring distance
I hear the C & O and Grand Trunk
Western trains torqueing slowly through
unmarked crossings. And hot yellow
cars winding up tight to red line

on the back roads out of here. My God.
All of us, everyone, looking for
a state of grace or the state line,
whichever comes first before morning.

Jack Ridl (b. 1944) grew up in western Pennsylvania. He now lives in Holland, Michigan, with his wife Julie and teaches at Hope College. His work has appeared in *The Georgia Review, New York Quarterly, Southern Poetry Review, Three Rivers Poetry Journal, Pennsylvania Review, Laurel Review,* and *Salmagundi.*

A Father

I remember how he'd wait; he'd
make a mound of peace and surround
himself with nothing
I could know. His mind
seemed alone at the taut end
of a kite string. I would wait,
hoping for the air to open dipping
him back to us. His eyes were empty,
sockets of morning light. I was on
my own, trying to learn at the end
of my fingers what it was he knew.

Growing Up American

I believed in Jesus and all the angels.
When the going got tough, in they'd come,
take me by the hand and lead me
down the hall, or through the night.
I knew how to pray,
and could feel the Lord's sweet presence
as I laid my errors at His feet
and prayed my enemies would keep
their eyes and fists away,
and begged that somehow Jeannie's dad
would leave his whiskey on the shelf,
and thanked Him for the life he'd given me.
I was taught that I did not deserve
the food I ate, my bed, the A's I got in math,
the basketball.
But now I wonder
if I also don't deserve
the emptiness between the stars,
the news that Uncle Paul is dead, the days
that go on into days.
One night each week,
my radio would catch
Buddy Blatner and his Hawks.
Alone, in bed, I'd listen:
imagine that slippery elm, Bob Petit,
at the line, holding the ball against his ear
while handsome Cliff Hagan,
whose hair held its part throughout a double overtime,
poised himself for an uncommon miss,
and Slater Martin,
fly weight street fighter stood behind the key.
I'd fall asleep at the foul line, dreaming
of 30 point games and a god who didn't care.

The Way It Is

Jesus, coming in the back door
with a knife and a summons
and a slice of pizza, sends us
all falling over our cards. He

looks each of us over, wipes his nose
on his sleeve and takes a bite from
the pizza. We are sweating. Outside
a car squeals and the neon light

in front of Johnny's Bar blinks red,
yellow; red, yellow; red, yellow.
I had been holding a royal flush.
I am fed up. This intrusion is too

typical. The night has always been
the time we loved each other best;
the only place we get along is here
at the table, with our booze, our

best cards, our lonely jokes and
reminiscences. Some old lady rents
the place to us, once a week. We
wait for it; now this.

Heaven

Groucho guards the gate, more
bewildering than God in judging
supplicants. Behind him Harpo, his hair
reason enough to realize there's nothing
we can do. "Say the secret
word." "Logos!" we shout. Groucho taps
his long cigar. "What?" he laughs.
"Logos!" "Logos? What the hell
is logos?" We are terrified.
We look to Harpo; he smiles, shrugs,
honks his horn, pulls some celery from his coat
and gnaws. Groucho lights
a new cigar, arcs his eyebrows, moving
the clouds of heaven higher, then looks
so sadly at us that we ache
to know what we have done. He turns
his back, catches sight of a lovely blonde
and slinks his way away, healing the sullen,
turning loaves and fishes into parakeets and somehow
pulling us through into the madness
of eternity.

Prayer on a Morning My Car Wouldn't Start

I sit behind the wheel
And finger the keys like a rosary.
Surely there is some prayer
That can move pistons.
If spirits slaughter germs,
Or bring about a sudden burst
Of hope or courage, even love,
Why not something simple, something
Closer to expedience? Why not dispatch
One lonely angel to caress my carburetor,
Fix my fan belt, or unclog my fuel line,
Just one greasy-winged mechanic,
Inept at saving souls, but damned
Good at getting me on my way.

Herbert Scott (b.1931) teaches at Western Michigan University. His books are *Disguises* (1974), *Groceries* (1976), and *Durations* (1984).

My Father's Bulldogs

1.

My father bred bulldogs on Pickard Street.
Our neighbors learned to hate us.
As many as a dozen animals growling and barking.
Misshapen dwarf-dogs, tongues askew,
flies boiling from excrement.

And vicious locked battles in the street.
My father at work.
My mother and my older sisters prying jaws apart
with brooms and mop handles.

Later, exhausted brutes wheezing and moaning.
Crodie, the family pet,
on the back porch, vomiting
behind the wicker clothes hamper.

2.

One night someone slipped into our garage
to tap in the heads of a new litter with a hammer.
Like a cook cracks eggs.

You always think you know who does something like that.
The unemployed brothers who live across the street
and down with their mother, next door to the house
of the young girl bitten by a black widow spider.

3.

My father brushed the bulldogs' coats for hours,
his quiet, Saturday ritual,
trimmed their thick toe nails,
taped their ears into roses.
As if *any* human labor could make them beautiful.

I loved Albert Payson Terhune whose dogs were sleek
and lovely, collies with finely tuned heads
who moved like thoroughbred horses. Or dogs

who were half-wild, fathered by wolves,
who became civilized for the love of a human.

4.

My younger sister, Addie, buried Crodie (alive) in her sandbox,
trimmed his ears with blunt-nosed paper scissors.
(Crodie wincing ever-so-slightly, apologetically.)

It was my fault Crodie killed our Easter chickens.
I left their shoebox in the back yard.
My sisters, forgiving, let me attend the funeral.

5.

In my room, perched on the edge of the bed,
my mother and father, embarrassed, in straight chairs,
doors closed on older sisters, I failed
What Every Young Boy Should Know.

So my father, shy in sexual matters,
took me to the garage
to watch him breed the bulldogs.

Those hushed evenings, my father's arms
around the bitch holding her steady
as Crodie circled, coughing, sniffing,
until his cock hung slick and limber.

My father, finally, taking the pendulous cock in his hand
to work it in before the fist-sized knot could form.
Crodie's soft black jowls leaking a satisfied drool.

6.

Driving to dog shows late at night with my father
through Oklahoma, Kansas, Missouri, the wing
windows of the Pontiac cranked open,

a stream of air across our faces,
ice-cold Coca-Colas from late-night diners
or vending boxes at filling stations.

Riding in silence through the dark passage of country,
smelling the languid, unclothed land, pungent,
like the body at night, opening, the held heat rising.

Herbert Scott

Hearts

"I prefer the dark meat," Mother says,
"so much more flavorful."

"Moist, delicious," Grandmother says.

Father and Grandfather love breast and wishbone.

"Brother loves the heart,"
these women croon, my sisters, too.

Chicken heart, goose heart, duck heart, turkey heart,

"Come to the kitchen, Brother,
your heart is ready!"

Oh, steamy heart gleaming on a white plate.
Jewel, crown, mouthful of joy—
how they sing its praises!

And I, most favored of boys, come
to that warm, stirred room
and chew the heart down.

Leonora Smith (b. 1945) is a poet and fiction writer. She was born in Great Falls, Montana, grew up on a farm in western New York, and now lives in East Lansing. She is a former editor of *Labyris*, has published in many little and literary magazines, and has a poetry chapbook, *Eating Red Meat*. She was awarded a Michigan Council for the Arts grant for fiction in 1983.

Photo by Robert Turney

from **Some Came Home**
for D. (1949–?)

Longing, we say, because desire is full
of endless distances.

Robert Hass

I. Missing in Action

The dark hours hunch
across the low fields, muster
in creek beds and sump holes
while our neighbors
sleep among tag ends of regret, the crusted
casserole dishes sent, emptied
and then carted home by their two boys—
as gawky and awkward,
in beards and suddenly civilian clothes
as they were three years ago,
shaved naked
from boot camp.
Their sleeves
seem to have shrunk overnight
and the flesh below their cuffs
seems blindingly white. Such light
could explode me.

I wear black
to absorb light, for fear
my honed and sparking edges
will slice through
what is left of the world.
Absence
is only the negative of presence,
equally real, but requiring dark,
a photograph coming up
in developer, a drowned girl
afloat just beneath the surface
of a farm pond.

Can you feel me
here, stripped of intention, hope,
but shakier than ever with desire?
It is all that I have now,
pure gesture, simple as the dog's breath
at the foot of the bed, the motion
of reaching to hold the space
where you were, or are.

II. Letter from a Muck Farm

Muck land, black as char, good
for root vegetables. The asparagus
has gone to seed, shoulder height, ferny
and tropic. The air is as clean
as if the moon has washed it. This
is where I come from, land
you might never see: thick, alluvial,
clumping in the hands, fields marked off
by hedgerows where the deer dodge hunters
in season, driven from their companionable
grazings among the cattle.

Once through this field
I let a boy take my horse's reins
as a Pony Express rider might lead a second mount
or run from bandits with a body
tied and slung across the saddle. It was another
who kissed me in that cherry orchard,
a night like this when the moon made shadows,
but earlier in the year, blossoms riding the sky
like snow clouds. I don't know why I came back here.
Perhaps I confuse you with all
I have ever lost, the one who leaped
to ride double behind me, hands
on my hips, creaks of a saddle, leather
smooth with regular use.

I have never seen your place, cannot name
the streams, the growth that might brush you
if you walked out your door and turned

in this direction, know nothing of your weather.
But look at that moon, how my arms
are lacy with the shadows of asparagus.
There is comfort in this place, a sense
that you are nearer here. Near enough at least
to see the same moon, though at a different
hour of the night, to have your face and arms
patterned by the same shadows, though laid
by a different vegetation, the crops
of a strange, lighter soil.

. . .

IV. Perspective

He has receded into distance
like the smallest fence post
in the drawing of a child
who has just learned
perspective,
tiny, almost invisible. No more
than a dot.

It is not so much
forgetting as the foreground
taking over, bushes sprouting,
the children climbing in and out
their upstairs window, the moon
the bowl of a spoon pouring light
over them like good cream. The man
holding the straining team of horses.
All this bustle, time and space
thickened with work.

The fence curves in front of the house,
the road snakes into distance. No road
could curve that far. Nothing
could be as far away as that dot,
and yet be the point

Leonora Smith

from which everything—the gold hoops
in my ears, bricks and slat boards,
all these tumbling children—
comes spilling, spilling.

Post Office: 1952

She stands against the wall
smoking a Lucky Strike,
wearing a red suit, now a little shabby,
featured four years before
on the cover of *Vogue*, tailored
by a man who once made uniforms
for the Luftwaffe.
The clerk flickers
behind the post boxes,
a sepia film through the yellowed glass.
His arm moves,
letters flick diagonal at numbers
but not into the box she watches
for the letter
that says where to write,
where to meet him,
what to tell the FBI.
That he loves her
and the daughter
who hopscotches
the floor's marble squares.
The woman's tongue darts,
her finger catches a shred of tobacco
as the clerk disappears,
sorting done. Her high heels click
like her lipsticks,
ring of keys.
She unlocks a tiny door
at the level of her daughter's eyes.
"You look," she says.

Through the square
the daughter sees distance,
room after room
of shelves stacked with packages,
bundles of mail.

Richard Tillinghast (b. 1940) grew up in Memphis and is now teaching at the University of Michigan. He is the author of three books of poetry: *Sleep Watch* (1969), *The Knife and Other Poems* (1980), and *Our Flag Was Still There* (1984). He has reviewed poetry extensively for the *New York Times Book Review,* the *Washington Post,* and *The Nation.* He has taught at Berkeley and Sewanee, and before coming to Michigan, he was Briggs-Copeland Lecturer on poetry at Harvard.

Photo by Chase Twichell

Allen's Station: They

The stars cool their fires in the river of night.

The big people sleep.
I step out barefooted onto the dewy, rough-boarded porch
And open my eyes among farm buildings.
Their yellow pine boards and whitewash
Illuminate my way.

Down the kitchen-garden path, through the orchard,
All the way this side of the leaning barn
Where the horses shuffle and snore,
Past a slumbering bull in a meadow,
Past the for-once-quiet chickens

I pad over velvet dust,
Through heady stands of ragweed,
Past the cooks' cabin
Where Kate and Aunt Martha
Have lit the morning lamp already
In their sturdy, square cabin
Wallpapered with years of the Sunday comics.

Orphan Annie's eyes
Never narrow or squint
Like Aunt Martha's do
And Dick Tracy is forever in profile
And will never look straight at lame, hobbled Martha
Who was born a slave
And because her church is on the property,
Has never left these acres.

And red-headed, Cherokee Kate
Who never has a civil word for *no one*
But Uncle Frank—Why is that?—
A different kind of uncle,
A cousin more like, if the tree were drawn.

Dagwood blunders across these walls
And will do so in his Bumstead way
Until the paper peels—
And Blondie with her thirties frizz

Is out shopping again
And will again commit the crime of unthrift;
And Major Hoople in his quilted dressing gown harrumphs,
Fires up his Meerschaum pipe
And sums up his opinion of life at Allen's Station:
"Egad!"

George A. and his wife and her sister and her sister's husband
And her three children, and Napoleon,
And a walleyed Indian-looking woman with a corncob pipe,
And some people I don't recognize,
Are going to the fields today to chop cotton.

Their blue overalls bleached to the ghost of white,
Their streaming Mason jars of well-water,
Their readiness for whatever reasons to work twelve hours
In the West Tennessee sun—
People today don't look like them, or talk like them.

The whites of Napoleon's eyes are purple.
Later in the morning, when he feels a little better,
He'll tell me again about the penitentiary
And show the healed, pink bullet-hole in his arm.

I'm seven, the farmer's little cousin from Memphis.

The lug-wheeled John Deere tractor
Strains with its wagonload of people
And follows the sun up and over the raised L & N tracks
That divide our farm from Beverly's father's.

The land surrounds us with its life:
Not the soil only—the oaks and poplars and sycamores
And cotton plants, and birds and beasts,
And all of us a part of it:
The people who work it, the farmer who owns it,
The boy who watches.

At the end of August my uncle
Will flag down the L & N
And I'll ride it back to Memphis
Through the whitewashed towns and sparse farms

And be met in a car
At the big station built with cotton dollars,
And go back to school
And grow up and move away.

They stay in the fields.
I watch them chop cotton,
Drinking water from their jar—
And them not seeming to mind—
As the dense green cotton leaves burn
And the purple boll explodes to ripeness
And the sun describes its slow arc.

They chop cotton, and stay right where they are.

On the Road to San Romano
(after André Breton)

Poetry like love is made in a bed.
In her messed-up sheets the sun comes up.
Poetry lives in deep woods.

She has all the room she needs.

One whole side of the universe

    Is ruled by a hawk's gaze,
    By the dewdrop on a furled fern,
    By the memory
      of a sweating bottle of Fume Blanc on a silver tray,
    By a thin blue vein down an obelisk raised over the sea.
    And the road of mental adventure, which peaks abruptly—
    One pause and it's weeded over.

No need to spread this around.
No need to frighten the horses.

    Shoals of salmon, hedges of songbirds,
    Rail-flanks opening before the approach of a railhead,
    Reflections from two banks of a river,
    The valleys baked into a loaf,
    The odd and even days of the calendar.

The act of love and the act of poetry
Are incompatible
With reading the news at the top of one's voice.

The way the sun shines,
The blue blur that binds the arc of the woodsman's axe—
The reach of a kite string,
The measured beating of a beaver's tail,
The diligence of lightning.
Someone tossing candies down
    from the top of an old staircase.

A good address is not necessarily part of the action—
Nor a corner office.
No, gentlemen—nor gin, leather, and cigar smoke.

Dance steps footed on a summer's night,
The shape of a woman's body delineated by throwing-knives,
Blown ephemeral smoke-rings,
The curls of your hair,
Slippery flutters of wettest flesh,
Ivy slithering into ruins.

The embrace of poetry,
like love's impossible, perfect fit,
Defends while it lasts
Against all the misery of the world.

Eric Torgersen (b. 1943) has taught at Central Michigan
University since 1970. His most recent book is the novella *Ethopia*.

Photo by Don Barber

What Is Your Earliest Memory?
What Does It Mean?
for Barbara Drake

Barbara the earliest thing I remember
is pushing a train of wooden blocks
sawed off the ends of two-by-fours
around the top of the concrete foundation
of the house my mother and father built
up Lyons Street at the end of the war.

It means we really were all there
together once, my father and mother,
my house, my brother and I,
my three sisters one after the other.

The foundation was a foundation
to hold up my little train
and I was a block and my brother
and sister and sister and sister.

I remember a little while later
my mother on the roof with a hammer.

The roof was a roof over our heads
but the house was never whole:
the bathroom no more than a shell,
around the back no shingles,
in the front yard a big stump
we had no one to dig up and haul.
We cut and tunneled and burned but the stump
was bigger than all of us together.

The stump was the stump of a tree
I can't remember. The tree was my father.

Eric Torgersen

Not Stopping

I have no place to go inside this mood,
but make no place for anyone riding shotgun.

You have the road, your thumb and sign,
an errand at a named place on the map;

I have this truck, mood, momentum, this nothing
to stop me, this no place to go.

Going and Staying
for Ann

I wouldn't go with you today,
swimming,
I chose to stay here

and to tell the truth someone
I hardly know
looked too good to me this morning;

but that it's good to be living
with you and have plans
is as true

and more useful;
the small
energy she raised

is liquid and convertible;
someone said
of the soul at death

it has no need to *go* anywhere;
staying at home
in a chosen life working

what energy I find
into poems
is my deepest day-dream;

love for you,
for poetry, the good
rich poems of John Logan,

Stroh's beer,
a little of which stays with me
though I piss it away;

this is my running,
my laps
in the pool, ten miles

on the ten-speed;
I'm feeling exalted, only
a little drunk, thinking

of you with no need
for my thoughts to go anywhere;
in earnest, in our own

good time we'll go places together;
the one need to leave
each other for long

is death, the need
not to *be* anywhere,
to pull up the plastic

sheet on the Magic Slate,
to shake the Etch-a-Sketch;
what if that need

comes to me right on schedule,
long before
it's scheduled to come for you?

It's time
to come clean, these are wedding
thoughts in a wedding

poem, death
is the need for a wedding;
young moderns who refuse

to die all want divorces,
their "freedom," not to have
to have children;

one girl wrote
to *Rolling Stone* she was saving
that energy for hiking at sixty,

at seventy, at eighty;
energy saved
in that bank gets lost in the crash

though we ride our bikes
at ninety,
ninety-one, ninety-two;

for now here's a ten-
mile poem, here's twenty laps,
not from need

to go but from pleasure
in going, being able,
from pleasure in staying;

I go this far today
and may never go faster
as you may not

on your slick
new Japanese bike
and so what?

if the going
and staying are one,
the coming together and parting.

Rodney Torreson (b. 1951) grew up on a farm in Iowa and currently lives in Grand Rapids. His poems have appeared in *Arete: The Journal of Sports Literature, The Beloit Poetry Journal, Great Lakes Review,* and *Passages North.*

Photo by Mary VanderMeulen

Dreams Should Not Dog Great Centerfielders

who come in from the pasture.
Dreams should be pets gone fat.

In nightmares Mantle is
cramped, broad shouldered,
in a taxi, hungry
as Mutt, his father,
who pitched his free time
to get Mick a ticket
from the mines.
He's late for the game, always.
       And Dimaggio at the airport,
despite his tall grace,
eyes darting like some terrier's
as he stands beside his luggage,
glances at his watch;
he is late, as if he's waited years
to board a flight
that takes him back
to Marilyn.

And Mantle's dreams
can't shake the guards.
The announcer says,
"Now batting . . . number 7,"
as Mantle finds a hole
in the fence
but can't squeeze through.
       And Dimaggio
for twenty-one years
sends six red roses
three times a week
to her Hollywood crypt
but they're a dog's
nervous patter.

The dreams of the greats should
be tame, trained
to open and close a gate,
with Mantle strolling

his heaven in center;
Monroe on her toes,
smiling, leaning into
The Clipper's arms,
returning the roses of her
red lips.

Don Larsen's Perfect World Series Game
Yankee Stadium, October 8, 1956

Despite the fall, Eden buzzed
in one crowded brain cell.
In this big fifth game against the Dodgers,
Larsen, whose best pitch was to the girls
at the bar, stepped toward the mound,
anxious to atone for his Brooklyn start,
hoping his mom in San Diego would watch
when he unwittingly heard God's warning:

"In the garden eat any fruit, but not
from the tree of evil and good."
Then he who broke curfew,
whose car once lost it at 5 a.m.
and wrapped around a telephone pole,
he who'd eaten from the wrong tree,
turned over control.

Though throngs circled him and teammates
smacked their gloves, God said,
"It isn't right for Don to be alone,"
and then put big Don Larsen to sleep
before the first pitch.
Then God reached into him for a rib
and formed a sweeping curve
to make his change of pace tail away.

And this was more than Larsen gave his wife
who filed this day to have his share
attached by the court, and with a snort
Larsen faced the mighty trees
of the Dodger bats, to avoid them like alimony.

For the Yanks Mantle homered, ran down
Hodges' drive. In mid game, perfection remiss,
Larsen felt pressure and a snake hissed
in every swing: "Larsen, give in.
Be the uneven pitcher you've always been."

How lovely and fresh a basehit would look.
And Larsen, nervous, toed the rubber
and felt it nub up in his legs till he
almost fell. But through the crowd
he heard the river of Eden roar.

And in the ninth, Furillo flied to the wall
in right, and Larsen gazed toward
the garden's edge, amazed at the leeway
within perfection, his pitches naked and unashamed,
and Campanella bounced to second.

Then Mitchell, the pinch hitter,
sidled up, sweet hits clustered on his bat
and the serpent bobbed: "Eat the fruit
of the basehit. Impeccability God bears not
in anyone but himself.
Eat before the Lord intervenes."

"Help me out, Somebody," Larsen moaned,
and two strikes branded Berra's mitt.
Then Mitchell fouled one off the crowd's roar.

"Here goes nothing!" Larsen sighed
and God, lonely for perfection,
looked no deeper than Larsen's words.
"Nothing it is!" God's voice rolled
and no ball was thrown, though Mitchell
saw a fastball, outside and low,
and the umpire a third strike
and Berra a mystery hard and white,
and with a leap Berra landed
in Larsen's arms and the crowd cheered
and cheered for their own lives,
and headed out the garden gate,
everyone feeling perfectly fine.

On a Moonstruck Gravel Road

The sheep-killing dogs saunter home,
wool scraps in their teeth.

From the den of the moon
ancestral wolves
howl their approval.

The farmboys, asleep in their beds,
live the same wildness under their lids;
every morning they come back
through the whites of their eyes
to do their chores, their hands pausing
to pet the dog, to press
its ears back, over the skull,
to quiet that other world.

In the Winter after Father
Lost His Hand in the Combine

The brooder door ajar,
the chickens,
as if to mock
the unwielded axe,
strutted into the snow
as though they had laid
their first abstraction.

They shook their combs
at the only words
they understood;
in a gust of feathers
flung themselves
upon the drifts
where they floundered.

The cold composed them
but in the morning
their only clear point
was at the end
of their foolish beaks.
Mother found them
frozen stiff, claws caked
to the branches
where they perched
in the trees,
eyes glazed
as if on the verge
of getting it right.

**After the Midnight Train Rumbles
through Staples, Minnesota**

you hear it, almost mothlike
on the porch screen,
all that's left
of the Burlington Northern,
a tremble in the mesh.

You imagine the whistle
feathered into antennae,
everything from engine to caboose
collapsed in a body
too faint to discern,

and wings, small as the
flickering thought
to a weary dispatcher
in a city too far from here
to matter.

Stephen Tudor (b. 1933) is a 1987 National Endowment for the Arts Creative Writing Fellowship winner. His book, *Hangdog Reef: Poems Sailing the Great Lakes,* will be published in 1988. He has published in *North American Review, Iowa Review, Michigan Quarterly Review, American Poetry Review,* and *Open places.* He teaches in the Department of English at Wayne State University, and is editor of The Hundred Pound Press.

Port Sanilac

Here's this earth girl—she likes
to get her feet wet, too—standing
croisé at the edge of Huron, that is,
standing in the third position and inclined
to the right as if listening for
her boyfriend's hand at the screen door
with her arms rounded and slightly
advanced from the body to make safe harbor
for boats bashed by the big lake.

I run into her just when it's getting dark.
And what kind of girl, what's her story?
Always lived in the same town—same house,
likes to look out at the ore boats,
favors barn dances, band concerts, picnics,
and, which I think is more important,
she is ample, lets you know you're welcome—
smiles, says hi, brushes her hair back, makes
fishing boats, cruisers, power and sail her own.

Although it is dark the attendants are
still on duty, saying we'll take your lines,
skipper; would you like a berth tonight?
And they hand *Aneirin* along the dock,
helped with the bumpers and tied her fast—
and when the boat is shipshape (with town so
close), I walk out for pie and coffee,
and the owner talks about a pond on his place . . .
the water as cold and clear as . . . first light.

Standing croisé at the edge of Huron her
eyes are the color of flax flowers, her hair
is straw, she is not fully awakened, is always
becoming. I'm not saying evil is tripped there
or the town's perfect. Was there but a short time
(cast off at half-past six the next morning),
but Port Sanilac, with her lapped seawalls,
her timbered docks, draws to herself the sailor,
let him test the wind, let ride the dark wave.

De Tour Village

1. *Bosley's Boat Yard (519) 297-3471; gas,*
diesel; transient moorage, electricity. ice;
haul-out to 35 tons, launch ramp, CB chan 11
monitored; hull repairs, gen mech. on duty;
courtesy car; tug service; restaurant,
laundry, groceries nearby.

But the place is a ruin: fallen docks,
Blasted workshed, junkfield, scurvy road's end—
And wildflowers, risen among the debris,

Thanks for them. For the few of them I picked
Go in water in a tumbler I've placed
In the gimballed drink-holder aft the tiller.

The common daisy and the black-eyed susan.
Head-proud, at ease beside the road;
Fireweed, thimbleweed, day lily, primrose.

Though I forget to water they last days,
And when I come to dock in towns I want
All to take notice: white clover, lupine

Chickweed, buttercup, bushy aster,
Meadow violet. Though winter comes,
Still blazing they linger in our eyes.

2. *Fred's Bar*

A "river room" next to the ferry slip—
Bar at back wall, a few tables, games.

Through the big window, the *P. R. Clark* upbound;
Drummond Dolomite on the other shore.

I call Detroit from phone near men's room.
The place depresses me. Bare, grimy, sad.

Wife says "don't talk so loud. They can hear you."
I'm whipped and filthy, myself. Comes the beer,

Barside, and there's this gaunt, toothless old guy,
Not quite drunk, and we talk about the lakes.

To see him you'd think he'd lived on the boats.
True, but just one year: 'forty-two to 'three.

A dock or loading cable crushed his leg.
That must have hurt like hell. *Naw. I passed out.*

Nine months with his leg up. He kept at me
About the mail boat: "What was that thing named?"

I couldn't remember, myself,
Starting to fly on the strength of one beer.

Then it came to him—the *O. F. Mook,*
Our only floating U.S. Post Office,

And after the *Mook,* the *J. W. Wescott.*
Shoots out below the Ambassador Bridge,

Runs up alongside ships, sticks bag
Into sky basket, takes on new mail.

That's my poetry, and she's still going strong.
That's my metaphor, after all these years.

3. *The Village Inn*

> *"The four saddest words*
> *That were ever composed*
> *Are these dismal sounds—*
> *THE BAR IS CLOSED."*

Still feeling punchy from the long, wet day,
I plunk down on the stool nearest the door.
It's supper time. The long bar's empty now
Except for a threesome at the far end:
The boss-lady, her waitress, a patron
Having a good laugh at someone's expense.
The place is dark, warm, gay with the lit speech
Of beer signs: blue green, red, softly obscene;
Medallions, teams of horses, waterfalls,

A comfort to the eye. "They sent me here . . ."
I venture. "From down below—don't I know,"
The old gal says. I order up. She pours.
My image in the mirror behind the bar
Stares back at me through a kind of glass waste:
Whiskey bottles, gin, vodka, schnapps, rum.
About the walls, words of advice: *today*
Is the first day of the rest of your life.
I know, I know, I promise to do better.
And now the young waitress brings my burger,
Thick, hot from the grill, oozing cheese,
Rank with onions, dripping with the red-brown
Slime of condiments and ground-round fat.
She's smoking. Runs her fingers through her hair.
Wants to know whether the food's o.k. "Great—
They don't have bars like this in Ontario."
None so vulgar. And none in such poor taste.
"Enjoy your meal," she tells me, wreathed in blue.
I wolf it down; I light one up myself.

Robert VanderMolen (b. 1947) grew up in Grand Rapids and
continues to live there. He is the author of six collections of
poetry, including *Circumstances* and *Along the River.* His work has
also appeared in *Epoch, Corona, Exquisite Corpse, New Letters,* and
Confrontation, and in *Scripsi* in Australia.

from **Estimates**

I.

Indians camped on shore—
Where the water is disturbingly clear,
Blue-tinted over stones, a postcard blue that draws you home,
Birch and blue, with acres of oak—

Wore bear grease
To hunt and scavenge roots and fruit,
Pine trails hushing along rivers to falls
To breaks where fires kept herds intact

Where lodges were later built
By entrepreneurs, that sagged
And rotted in 20 years

As clearings closed, like a string had been pulled,
And roads disappeared in a decade

With a sack of trout
The boy meanders cross-country
Keeping to higher ground, trees pushed over, bear droppings,
Meadows where dams washed out, beaver cuttings, brown and
        peeling

With no confessions, no compass, no ambition, no vanity,
Barrels stuck in leaves where horses were watered
Below a spring,
Small shacks tilted
Where porcupines had eaten through walls
And floors

    Wealthy men
Sailed up from Cleveland with attractive women
And boxes of religious pamphlets

Standing among the slender oaks,
The agitated oaks, powdery soil beneath their feet

Where the French had stood
With a purple document, thinking of the Rockies

III.

Everything changed color,
Richness sifted into the ground, kilns distintegrated into ruins
Along the Soo Line tracks, sawdust, breasts of sawdust, sank
Into themselves. The boy observed,
Keeping a spiral notebook. The hardware store was boarded up
Though the tavern expanded, as well as federal funds for the post
     office.
Simple enough. Maidens with wild cherry garlands
Danced down lanes of the high power lines

In black and white

Silver birds jittered across ruts and stumps

     Standing in snow
     Beech-hued the opening,
     In the silence of ravines,

     To where it's kicked up
     For nuts and ground cover

     Crows skidding over the maple tops
     Towards Hugh's Swamp

Moss in the Spring, with glades of fern resting in suspension,
Bear standing, sniffing and dreaming, melons and corn, of bacon
     cooking
In homemade trailers, men throwing dishwater out into snow

Said Simon, a Canadian who fought in the Korean War,
An Ojibway, who doesn't own a rifle, doesn't trust one,
Doesn't trust himself with one,
I woke up on the other side of the bridge next to Christmas, next
     to the highway,
But the judge let me go

I was going to my sister's, she makes Indian junk
From porcupine quills. I came back here instead

He ducked back into his trailer, between stacks of magazines,
To reappear with beer for us

IV.

Brown the wall of rock where the country descends abruptly,
The fallen timber brown

Virgin pine tufted out
And breezy, above the shoulders of hardwood,
Swaying
Everything swaying

Water hissing out of ice
Where the walls sweat ice

The stairs half built and mossy

    Frank
    Scrawling a map in sand
    Where the two-track turned into a minor canyon

    It used to be here, he said,
    Drawing a question-mark

My brother and I climb the hill
A pinnacle
Where our grandfather said you could see
In the old days an Indian trail
As clear as a vein running east

Before the logging

    Apprizing the slope,
The weather, hemlock where deer bedded in snow

The snow falling in great clots,
Then the void

Robert VanderMolen

How swiftly one grows vulnerable

In Hugh's Swamp
Black ducks idling in black water

In Hugh's Swamp
The remains of a small gauge train that fell through ice

Farm House

Your muscles take a long time to grow tame again

    Ah, the scent of marigolds
    Kneeling in them
    Crushing them

There is just the chair
Where you rock against an unfinished wall

With cornstalks and crows,
A detached illustration from a calendar

At 65 degrees,

And something about leather
The color, the memory of leather
Hauling wood on your sled to the kitchen for your mother

Ah, the beauty of neglect

    Hitting stones with a baseball bat
And watching them sail into the stony pasture

    You were born into an age that lost things
Than ran roughshod over real wood

That imagined loneliness
Was a dimness—a low-grade disease—

Not bright and cold

Ambivalance, not wildness

Not like the armies of Fall
When apples are ripe

    Under the porch
    Where you tossed things all summer

    They settled in

Robert VanderMolen

    That in itself
Is a pleasure, like cider, the taste and color of cider

Like the sky heading south, and all the trucks
Rumbling dust past the barn

Diane Wakoski has lived in Michigan and taught at Michigan State University where she is the Writer in Residence, since 1975. Her most recent collection of poems is *Rings of Saturn*.

Photo by Robert Turney

A Snowy Winter in East Lansing

We feed the birds
leaving mixed corn and millet and sunflower seeds
in a big pole feeder,
thistle seed in two small tubes,
and pure sunflower kernels in a domed plastic globe,
but only the sparrows come, hundreds of them,
an occasional chickadee,
and one lonesome pair of finches.

After two years,
we no longer expect other birds, though
we long for flashing cardinals, noisy
blue jays, purple finches, towhees, downy
and hairy woodpeckers.

But in this part of the midwest,
the land is flat and monotonous,
there are no good restaurants,
and even our friends seem to leach out
each year, or become flattened
by the terrain. So,
                    I've stopped
believing that even the birdfeeders
could yield surprise
or drama,
or colour,
for that matter;
I like the life,
the sense that we've done all we can.
And the English sparrows,
sitting like little candles in the big
yew bushes, heaped with fluffy snow—
they have their beauty too,
if looked at,
with certain eyes.

Diane Wakoski

The Map of Michigan

is in the shape
of a mitten. Only the thumb
articulated, the rest of
the fingers
bunched together under one knitted pocket. This hand
or one so sheathed
could not
play the piano
or perform most of the tasks that created
our civilization.
The thumb,
we are told,
gave primates a head start,
but without the slender muscled fingers, man could
never have come so far.
The mittened hand can chop wood,
go fishing, build
a fire, be a catcher's mitt,/
but where is poetry and music
in this early dumb hand?

Waiting, of course,
for the glove,
fine sensuous leather from needled Spain, Morocco, or Mexico,
hot skin to change our lives
        —The King of Spain to place
        a diamond ring (every woman's dream)
        on this newly revealed
        finger.

Danae
for Thomas McGrath

It was a shower of g(rain),

dust and chaff flying through everything,
the wheat pits winking like fireflies in the North Dakota
hot, harvest air.
                    The end-summer night fields
burning with radiance, as threshing continued past
darkness, pale yellow lemonade for parched voices,
the men covered with a dusting
of this golden flack.
                    How could a girl
not see them as Gods, their arms and backs
swelling with muscles and covered with
gold?   How could a woman
resist making love, if Cal or his protege, Thomas,
could come showering this glittering grain-rain
of abundance on her? Bread forever
to eat, on the lips, burnished and glowing but soft as peaches
    broken
open on the ground?
                    How could she want
to be apart from this litany of swirling, showering, shooting-star
light, of wheat and stalks and dust, all pulsing and reflecting
light, dazzling
light, twirling
light, the stars turning on the Christmas tree,
the chips of light and ice, shivering and circling around Saturn,
    coating
the moon, dusting the lips, wet with sweat,
the arms and backs with coiling gold muscles
from light, from
so much light, how could she
not
embrace this golden rain transforming her body
into a trumpet, the insides of a transparent piano, a harp;
nothing Beethoven or Mozart wrote EVER could be so beautiful,
so stippled and engraved, encrusted and merged
with light.

Diane Wakoski

Sapphires & Emeralds in the Mail

An aging boy blown into a giant mollusk
    riding his snail bicycle madly, the frame bending
    under his poundage, his backpack bulging with used books,
convinces me
this town drives people crazy.
His silky mind is frayed and stained
like a blanket thrown in a ravine. He wants
to play a game of chess with
everyone
to prove he's smart, when we all know
he's smart; want him to move out of the house
with his nurse mother and his violent brother,
get a job and at 38 stop ranting
about snobs, demographics and evil book dealers.

Once a month I win a sapphire or emerald
as I enter all the free contests
that come in the mail,
fantasizing blackjack in Atlantic City casinos,
and talking slot machines in Las Vegas,
but in fact what I win is pin-points of carbon,
black with a white streak somewhere,
and dull green little nubs like pencil erasers
that come in plastic bags
saying "Genuine."
They are, I guess; but what to do with 11 black dots
and now about 5 dull green erasers?

My wall is papered with further announcements
that I am a definite winner of yet another
Tamiz Emerald (or Cuisinart;   VCR;   Color TV),
but those bigger prizes never arrive. Only month by month
these tiny dull stones, like spots of spinach left on a dirty plate.
It is the midwest,
I keep saying. Your luck here
is confined. The boy who carries his snail-house-life on his back
has stopped doing anything
but gaining weight and riding his strained frantic bike. He
    doesn't
even try to win

these birdseed sapphires
or smaller than a dried pea emeralds.
He's stopped hoping envelopes will arrive
addressed to him,
with awards, or even from lovers or friends.

I wait to win, while
he waits to be run over, or die.
Sapphires, emeralds, death:
You are a definite winner of one of the above.
I wait for mine to come
in the mail.

Rayfield Waller (b. 1960) is a resident of Detroit's lower East Side.
His work has appeared in *Solid Ground and Nostalgia for the
Present: An Anthology of Writings from Detroit*. He has been editor
of *Wayne Literary Review*.

Photo © 1987 by S. Kay Young

from **Search for the Missing Ellipse**
for Esperanza Malave Ciutron

2.
the south
i seem to see my grandfather moving like a tank
thru red mud
shotgun resting like a lover on his shoulder
a scar there where the shotgun has rested so many years
his brother beside him
with a small .38
crickets sneering as they glance at the moon
the moon is orange, bright
too bright
beause they can be seen   [you, grandfather, can be seen
                    and when a white man calls from a
                    farmhouse
"WATCHOO NIGGUHS DOIN OUT THEUH THIS TAHMUH
    NIGHT??"
your brother freezes
his fear makes him curl his toes inside the muddy boots
his scrotum contracts
but you, my grandfather, you just smile and spit
(that crazy smile, the crazy way of yrs when you were young)
"WE JUSS HUNTIN NIGHT RABBIT, MISTUH CROSS. YOU
    WANNA JOIN US??"
then you laugh and walk on
"DUKES, YOU CRAZY?"
yr brother hisses at yr back
"slavery gone"
you simply say
and you pull on thru mud, leaves and bush
and you worry
and the next time you hear a rustle from behind
you feel yr heart sink
but you are not afraid]

3.
the north
i seem to see my uncle moving like a gyroscope
across the scarred cement

his step is bebop his cloth coat limp with the rain
a harmonica resting like a lover in his pocket

[in the mist of the 50s, my uncle, did you
doowap on corners with niggers more raggedy than you?
you inherited yr father's indian nose—did they ask about that?

when hoppin at the 20 Grand
leaning on the thighs of hosts of women
who wanted to love you
you looked into the lenses of scores of cameras
that followed the ellipse of yr smile
but failed to capture yr eyes
the women right next to you
but yr eyes somewhere else

mamma's boy
sissy writing song lyrics another stubborn Dukes boy
who conked his hair because his father told him not to

under
a full orange moon, a swollen moon   floating like
a cynical old man above Dexter street
you are fighting cops, cops who wear gas masks
that make them look like 6 ft. insects
a national guardsman in a tank
kills yr best friend
you are struck in the head

and you wake in a musky cell
you feel yr pockets desperately for the harmonica
and yr heart sinks
but you are not afraid]

For Joe Louis

twice
this fat man
has driven his knuckles
into the side of yr face
yr kidneys are swollen
the back of yr neck
is sticky with blood
            before the fight
the newspaperboys all smiled at you
they called you
"TAN TARZAN OF THUMP"
and had you sit for photos
with their little girls
on yr lap
and you forced yrself to smile
into the exploding flashes

twice
this fat, german bastard
has splattered yr blood
into the grinning faces
at ringside
twice
he has battered yr head almost
cracking yr skull

somewhere a crowd is roaring you hear it
as if you are under miles of ocean you
see bright yellow flashes a woman's breasts
dance in yr memory as you see the mat rush up
at yr face you taste the canvass STAY DOWN
you hear somebody shout

but you don't

For John Clare

to be human has its price
here, in the shadows of cathedrals and clocks
here, beside the river flowing nowhere
here, at the roadside where you were penniless
here, where you yanked at patches of grass
here, where you walked in gloom
here, in High Beech asylum behind walls
here, where you rubbed sore eyes
here, where dank stone would sweat
here, in the heather and the gloam you found
that to be human has a price
here, on the cobbled ways of London
here, in the sitting rooms and courtyards
here, beside the river flowing nowhere
here, in the shadow of the wealthy
                    you remember
you remember barnyards and alfalfa, pastures
remember hounds crying after sunset
remember forests of dew, horses stinking in the steaming rain
remember armies of owls about the farm
remember hunger like a wound you suffered at birth
    and carried here
here, where dank stone would sweat
here, beside the river flowing nowhere
here, in St. Andrew's asylum behind walls
here, where the sun will cross the sky
here, where you pace the cold halls
here, in weak moonlight
here, with a blanket on your cot behind you
here, with a box beside you, a casket of poems
                    you scratch at wooden doors
and you listen to the echos.

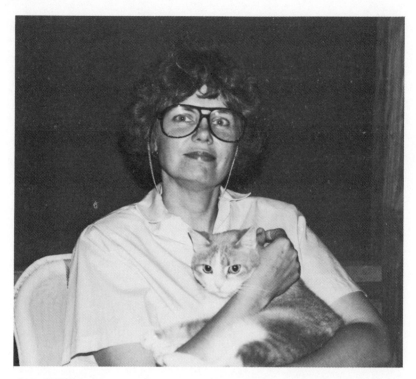

Ann Williamson was born in 1943 and grew up in Cincinnati, Ohio. She now lives in St. Joseph with her husband and three sons and works as a registered nurse. Her work has appeared in *Earth's Daughter, Currents, The Mickle Street Review,* and *The Green River Review.* In 1987, she received a grant from the Michigan Council for the Arts.

The Angel

When the angel passed over town,
townspeople heard a great rush,
as of wings, and a whole tree
of grackles flowered up to heaven.
Standing in her kitchen, one woman
saw the air bloom wings.
But just out of town,
the October lake was quiet—
a school of drab leaves
breathless on the surface,
a rubbish of colorful fins
motionless on the bottom,
and pondweed deadlocked
along the shore. The unsettled
grackles shuttled over the water,
and the image of the angel
struck the lake. Eccentric
ripples circled from the impact.
The drab leaves trembled down and up,
their veins prefiguring gills
and fanning the water for dissolved
lights. The image passed,
and the leaves remained
in their allotted places.
The unnecessary complication of wings
churned droplets, obscuring
the ruckus of the bottom
where colors were set in motion
but did not advance.
When the angel passed over the lake,
there was a quickening tempo
of weed along sand, and a small stand
of aspen blossomed with the squabble
of grackles. Stirring in her kitchen
one woman saw soup bones leap in the soup.

The Hummingbird
for Ann Mctavish

The only moving
thing was the eye
of the blackbird.

—Wallace Stevens

The barn is an old sock
darned at the heel.
One thing worth noting
is a scrape of red behind it.

I love two women—
the housewife tying red cloth
to her porch every morning
and the one untying it at evening.

Doubts assailed her on the seventh day.
She threw a pinch of red over her shoulder.

I cook all month
like a bride with one recipe,
simmering twenty red days
stirring up hummingbirds.

Behind the speck of barn,
an acre of red,
this attracted the eyes of two hummingbirds.

The hummingbird that stayed away twenty days
was colorful as the one appearing on the twenty-first.

Across the highway
I begin my novel about a barn
and a red heart.

The hummingbird no housewife seeks
is merely a hummingbird
The housewife no hummingbird flys to
is merely a housewife.

Along the Davenport Arms

Along
the davenport
arms and back
among
the cushion
chinks and upon
Your chintz lap,
the quanta are purring
and snarling while You
doze, Mother.
They hackle
and nuzzle, mating
then, like as not, spit
apart, and Mother, You who
are like Death always counting,
You blink and lose track of them,
two, four, six . . . many,
or You count furiously
one pair of them again and again.
They are all the same to you,
Mother, they are all the same.

Virtual quanta come into existence in pairs, then annihilate each other before nature counts their lifetimes. Thus the law of conservation of energy remains intact.

Ann Williamson

Tomatoes

August is heat, miles thick,
moving over the low browns
of the garden, leaving tomatoes
too ripe on the ground.
There are too many tomatoes—

My mother is putting them up.
They are such stupid kittens
she doesn't even tie them in bags
just drops them into the water.
They bob up and down, mewling.

She has scalded her glassware, jars
dry over their own heat, their metal
clamps sprung. We are tasting, she holds
the spoon, the wooden handle, she only
has to turn around to reach me.

All afternoon a glacier of sun
gouges basins of light
into the windowsill's white paint
and pushes tomatoes into red
heaps of boulders.

They are for supper.
My mother runs them under the faucet,
the yellow smell washes off their skins,
and I want her to stop,
but she does an amazing thing—

turns on the stove, forks a tomato
roasting it over the burner.
The skin shines like red
patent leather over
the foot of a fat baby

dressed up on the worst day of summer.
Skin splits from the fork,
from the metal prongs, comes off
all of a piece. My mother
slices tomatoes onto a plate.

John Woods (b. 1926) was reared in southern Indiana. He served
in the Air Force in World War II. Since 1955, he has taught at
Western Michigan University, where he was appointed
Distinguished Faculty Scholar. He was named Distinguished
Michigan Artist in 1978, and was a National Endowment for the
Arts Fellow in 1982. He is the author of eight books of poetry, the
most recent being *The Salt Stone: Selected Poems* (1985).

Long Days and Changing Weather

Late afternoon in mid-August, the day settles back.
The children nap, the needles of their tongues
buried in cloth. Dogs survey their endowments
under the shade oaks. They are sincere.
Cash registers never sleep, you know,
and there are lovers who roll back under
the roaring air conditioner. They feel
they have been stroked by two cold hands.
Even the wind has a coarse weave.

This is human scale, endearing, saddening,
what two eyes can see, what sixty years can recall.
In late afternoon in mid-August,
neutrinos plunge through the earth,
What Has God Wrought nears Pluto,
and we are invisible to certain white cats.
Insects, birds live and die
in exotic explosions, and the shade oaks
have traded groin art for time.

The children rouse. Their needles pierce
elder ears. Why do they scream death
when they most enjoy? The dogs look up,
their ears on different levels.

The lovers have showered again.
They come down to begin the supper,
food that has come through so many stars,
so many gullets and roots,
before it found its table shapes
and household names.

Poetry Seen As the Shuffling of Stones

Small, sodden computor, the poet
is counting again. This is a day
when power has not come down the lines.
It has rained a week, and there are things
growing in the back yard
I would not speak to, but the meters
aren't turning. I haven't lost a lover
for a week, and our wise men
haven't discovered the Vegetable Brain,
though I am in the turnip stage.

I pull close my jar of simples,
the box of lost mesmers and spirit knuckles.
And then the stones. Here's the agate
that squared the circle in the cinders
behind the grade school.
Here's the timerock from the meteor
that mammalized the dinosaurs.
Here's the Pridestone,
on which I daily bark my shin.

There are those in my clan
who are disappointed by the dailies,
and track ancestors back to honor,
to position, maybe to the Stegosaurus.
Hear, in this Petoskey stone
wind the aisles and fonts,
the stations of crystallization.
Before the trilobite, before
the milkthread sporecase, before the birds
and bees heard about the birds and bees,
a god lounged at this shrine of fire
and curdled water, raised on elbows
of lightning, beard blowing down
the smoking scrags
and the lone pale drift of silicate.
Thank you, King James and your versions!

In southern jungles, we are told
there are stones laid out that speak

to the stars and their visitors.
We have lain in the damp grass
of a northern place
and have read the dreams of people
in the far ice stones of the sky.
How lonely for us, shuffling our palm-warmed stones
for peace and bewilderment.

Under the Lidless Eye

These are hunters.
In their season, they lurch down
from the camper through gray-crusted snow
to hunch ancestrally:
the shiver-and-shake of urination,
marking the clearing with steam.
They have license.

When trees rage and char,
when we fold silkskins into the camphor,
chewing dark fat, these men take down long bows,
the fowling pistols and skinning knives.
Some have painted on grease-smoked cave walls
and some pass Polaroids. Their necks rasp.
Their nails deepen to blue steel.
Hair springs out of their cheeks.

Then there is the war of the bumper stickers,
hatchbacks glaring at each other in parking lots.
Some say the over-and-under, the magnums
loosen the groin; that the women they have shrined
with dual accounts jackknife in their jibes:
wet notches, receiving chambers
for the oily rounds. They say that these men
are the barbers who, cable-necked,
bump chests at Little League. Evenings they clean
their weapons, easy in the kitchen liquidities,
men as they were. Later the children hear,
from their high beds, that there are traps
around the office water cooler, spear pits
beneath that strange, lurching animal, *family.*

Up near Houghton, the buck's head sharpens.
Grazers turn the long triangles of imagination
toward the camper radio. The song says
there is one clearing
where we always leave a little blood
because the weasel must eat, the owl must drift down
on the shrew, the deer swell with parasites.

Through this clearing and the next,
through the camper, the little recording booth
winding country truths, a music moves so slowly
even the oak can't hear it, even the oak
who gave up passion for time, through whose eye
the hunter's flesh seethes around
precise armatures. Blood without passion,
it tells. Death without processions.

Over this clearing, the moon rises,
once the Huntress in the youth of her praisers.
When her eye opens, all our fats and colors
fry out. She can see cells detonate
and the long carapaces of lake ice.
She sees the hunter lift his taut bow,
the buck raise his heavy rack.
She sees compasses bowing at consecrated text.
Yes, she can make one white stone
burn in the stream bed,
but she makes the shadows darker.
We do not know who watches the moon.

The Fourth Morning in September
(for Dave Pugh, in 1986)

Time is a bomb. The old barns of the county
lean on whatever can take it. There's shrapnel
in the corners of our eyes. That's all right.
The scythe is a clear clock, counting
the gathering with the winnowing.
Though we wore a Ruptured Duck and other honors,
no stewing hen has ever understood
why we took down the good silver
on a Sunday in September. Bless the table
and the dumplings and the linen,
stiff as silver. But we ate our blessings
instead of counting them, becoming
thick and weathered as barrels.

But what do we do on Sundays
when the Lord don't hear nobody pray?
The scent trails out for all hunters.
Today, if you climb up on the windmill,
you'll see one crow, mangy-winged,
leading his cross shadow
over white fields that cover the combine.
Perhaps those are scarecrows near the barbed fence.

Since it is Sunday in our mother's house,
say a few words for the cows, for Spot,
(the dog's dog), for the hired hands,
trucked over from Morgantown,
glaring into the haying sun.
They all stood there
on the last Sunday of a world,
shadows burning into stone.

Someone was asked to dinner
who ate everything.

Terry Wooten, born in Cadillac in 1948, is a poet-bard in the oral tradition. He lives on a farm near Elk Rapids, where he has built and is host poet of the Stone Circle. He has taken his oral poetry program to thousands of students across the state. His books of poems include *Got In An Argument Over Harmony* (1978), *The 45th Parallel* (1983), *Okeh* (1984) and *Words Wild With Bloom.* His poetry is featured in *The Stone Circle Anthology* and in *Poets of the Stone Circle* (1984), an educational video.

Photo © 1986 by Elizabeth De Beliso

Crow Dance

On the road
out front of the house
a male crow does his spring strut dance
for a lady crow of his choice.
Daylight glistens brand new full of soft, damp colors.
The crow's shiny, black head bobs
up & down
to the mating rhythm
inside him.
He steps
real fancy,
a kind of march.
Lady crow pecks at the gravel
beside the road
watching him
out of the corner of her eye.

Story of Kewadin

The death of Kewaydin, last of the blue-blood
Chippewas, was a time of quiet celebration
among the Christian Indians, and those of the
old ways, too. No one knew exactly how old he
was, but it was common knowledge he'd fought
at the River Raisin Massacre on the British
side in 1813. It was the bloodiest battle in
Michigan, at least in modern people's memory.
The Little Big Horn pales in comparison. Of
the one thousand U.S. soldiers, only sixty
fought their way out, most of them Kentucky
sharpshooters. And old Kewaydin loved telling
stories about those who didn't make it.

After the war the animals seemed to prefer him.
Every spring, he had the biggest belly and the
tallest stack of furs. But like his name, The
Northwest Wind, Kewaydin could be just as surly.
In later years people said he went to work for
"Matchi Manitou," an evil spirit who lived on the
dark side of the moon. The Indians of Wequagemog
on the north edge of Elk Lake grew wary of him,
especially his beaver skin pouch full of tricks
and medicine. A patient people, they waited for
the days to sneak up on him one sunrise at a time.

But old Kewydin saw it coming. Two moons before
his death he converted to Christianity and lived
out his days with a smirk, in the sanctuary of
his daughter's home. He died in 1884 surrounded
by winter. They chiseled a grave in the ground
and sent old Kewaydin on his way with a bouquet
of dried flowers in one hand and his hunting
knife in the other, plus two extra white shirts
for the long trip through the hunting grounds
to the celestial city. And most important, a
long rope with a grappling hook on the end of it,
to climb over the wall into heaven, in case the
angels refused to let him in. A few years later,
they named the town after him.

Willie

By the end
Willie was nothing but
a knotty skeleton
lashed together
by stubborn old muscles
wrapped in worn out, burlap skin.
He was one of the last
of the old wolverines,
& he worked right up
to the final harvest
in his son-in-law's garden.

Willie had worked hard all his life
& wasn't afraid to say so.
When he said so
he'd get right up in your face,
& the words would fly
like a thrashing machine.
But he always had good breath
so it wasn't so bad.

Willie never had much money.
He just liked to plant things
& watch them grow.
In his heyday he never knew
much about birth control.
His family resembled a miniature city.
Out of necessity Willie became
pretty good at cutting corners.

This was back when
doctors still made house calls.

The doctor came again one night
to help out with another birth.
To give Willie something to do
he handed him his medical instruments
& told him to sterilize them
in some hot water.

A half hour later
the doctor couldn't
find his instruments anywhere,
& Willie was out in the barn.

The doctor had been
on the road all day
& was hungry,
so he helped himself
to some bean soup
simmering on the stove.
That's when he found his tools.

Willie had the only
daughter in the county
born with the aid of
medical instruments
sterilized in homemade bean soup.

Last Words of Max Ellison

So here I am on top the scrap heap
wired for plumbing. Excuse me if I cry
a little. I can't hide my feelings as
easy as I used to. Life is hard and I
guarantee that none of you will get out
of here alive either.
    I'm writing a poem about dying.
It'll be called "Fancy Pants," after
these diapers I'm wearing, but you
might have to finish it. If I get
any thinner or weaker, I'm going to
go right through the window. When I die
I'm going to a better place, and if I
don't like it there, I'm moving on.

Jan Worth (b. 1949) is a Flint social worker and has been a newspaper reporter and a Peace Corps volunteer to Tonga. Her work has been published in *Passages North, The MacGuffin, The Burning World, Moving Out, Brix,* and *Industrial Strength Poetry.*

Photo by Greg Brown

Lunch with the Mortician

Not all kinds of death can be repaired.
The drowning victims are beyond help
and there is not a single infant
whose death he can make beautiful.
But many of the bodies can be improved.
He is an artist. He does everything
himself. Next time you see someone
laid out, pay attention: are the hands
clean and folded neatly where they can
be seen? Are the clothes pressed
and in good taste? He can build up
a face and give it color, applying
cream and rouge. What they would have
given for such tenderness in life!
He files and polishes each nail,
down to the last pinky, and shapes
the hair, even glueing something extra
to scalps ravaged by chemotherapy.
This is for the family, he says:
they need to see their loved one
tended in death, no matter what happened
before. Try to think of it like this,
he says, smiling over our small
window table. If I did you,
it would be like your wedding:
you are in a trance, and you want
somebody to do everything for you.
I would wash you and dress you and
make you up. I would even take you
to church and arrange you
so beautifully that when your guests
came in they would not be able
to catch their breath.

He loves this work. Divorced, he goes up
each night to his apartment over
the mortuary, thankful he does not
have to eat his ex-wife's porcupine meatballs
any more. He spreads cold cuts and
gourmet mustard on a slab of rye,

settles down with good Scotch
and old Sinatra. It's a living,
he says, pressing his fine hands
together, an excellent life.

Canning Beans

Come inside, my mother says,
and leave the men to clean the beans.
It's time I tell you
what I know of canning.

I jump up as if
my slip is showing.
To get this old without knowing
cleaning beans is men's work?

We lean over the 1940s canning pamphlet,
elbows like rudders on the counter.
She touches each how-to intently,
as if to start from scratch.
Clean jars, she orders, and hot.
She twists a linen towel
around each neck. And try to find
linen—it's scarce.
And listen: your father
isn't always like you think.
Some things between us now,
they are almost a sacrament,
as if, after all, we are
married at last. When we
do dishes, he takes up all
the flatware in his big hands
and passes them over
to the hot water, and I gather them
in my small hands and lift them out
and he touches me.

She looks to see if I heard,
as if I am slow, as if she knows
she must say this in simple words
or I will be in over my head.
The air expands with insect whirr
and memory. I see my father out there,
snapping beans with my own man, nodding
in the green shade.

I got my dream, my mother says,
I'm old and unruly but
I waited him out. Your father loves me.
Now get to work, girl,
these beans are ready.

So we pack her crop against winter,
steam smoothing out our wrinkles,
the kind jars clanking.

Oregano and My Mother's Fall from Holiness

It was her first herb.
Thank goodness, she said, there's something
to put in food besides salt and pepper!
I just don't think I could take the boredom
another year of my life!
She didn't even know how to say it,
had us calling it ore-ee-GAN-o
for years, saying it
like world travelers,
proud we'd gone beyond staid roast beef
and Protestant potatoes.
She was our Marco Polo,
announcing her discovery in our food
like the arrival of a Chinese emperor.
She started making pizzas
to put it on,
thick-crusted monstrosities
that tantalized us all day,
dough rising thankfully for something
other than bread, and it would come out
smeared with tomato sauce and pepperoni
and everything sprinkled with
ore-ee-GAN-o
and we thought we had arrived,
had a little of the Armenian in us,
maybe had a funny last name.
Then she launched huge lasagnas,
steaming strata brought to table
in a battered roaster,
each meal her conquest.

Later we found out
we said it wrong, and held our tongues.
She grew her own chives by then
and had moved on to chili powder,
but these were never the same
as brave oregano,

Jan Worth

when we first heard
polka music late at night, red wine appeared
in thimblefuls, and even our father saw
she was done with Calvinism for good.

My Father Gives Me Stilts

Deep summer, the spots under the swings
already mud hard, he leans the stilts
against the barn for me to find. I swing out
from the cherry tree where I spent
that dreamy July, and he's watching
from the tractor when I grab the pine poles
wrong and fall over hard. I hear him laugh
that chesty laugh, slosh through
wet grass to show me how.
"Here, you grab them from the front,
you wrap your arms around like this!"
And off he goes, clomping down the road,
picking his big feet up off the gravel,
right through puddles, grinning back
where I stand in my skinned knees, clapping.
He yells, "Once I walked two miles
on these, just to see if I could!"

Then I learn, and I tower everywhere,
one whole summer better than the rest,
preferring my grand and awkward height
to the earth, "flittin' in the heavenlies
again," Mom says, her philosophy that
you have to come down sometime.

But two feet up I disagree, and Father smiles
from far off as I pole straight-faced
over black clods, cement blocks, everything.
To be like him whenever I choose, gaining
his stature on a whim! The mischief sticks,
and I almost never fall.

INDEX OF TITLES AND FIRST LINES

Poem titles are in roman type and first lines in *italics*.

Michael Delp is the Director of the Creative Writing Program at the Interlochen Arts Academy. In 1984 he received a Creative Artist grant from the Michigan Council for the Arts, and he has twice won the *Passages North* National Endowment for the Arts Poetry Competition. His poetry, fiction, and non-fiction has been published in numerous magazines, including *Poetry Now* and *Playboy*.

Conrad Hilberry is professor of English at Kalamazoo College. He received his B.A. from Oberlin College and his Ph.D. from the University of Wisconsin. His most recent book is *Luke Karamazov*, a psychological case study of a multiple murderer.

Herbert Scott is professor of English at Western Michigan University. He was a National Endowment for the Arts Fellow in 1984 and has received a Michigan Foundation for the Arts award and a Michigan Council for the Arts Creative Artist grant. He and Conrad Hilberry are two of the editors of *The Third Coast*, an anthology of Michigan poetry published by Wayne State University Press in 1976.

The manuscript was prepared for publication by Laurel Brandt. The typeface for the text and the display is Palatino, designed by Hermann Zapf. The book is printed on 60-lb. white offset paper. The cloth edition is bound in Holliston Mills' Roxite Vellum.

Manufactured in the United States of America.